"By sharing the timeless writings of the early Church Fathers, revealing their wisdom as well as their foibles, Mike Aquilina unveils the importance of friendships for the Church today. A fun read."

ROGER FINKE

Author of *The Churching of America* and Professor of Sociology and Religious Studies, Penn State University

"Mike Aquilina's *Friendship and the Fathers* is a book that elicits a conversion in the reader. In an age that considers adult friendships in particular to be marginal to our identities, Aquilina offers an account of friendship in the early Church integral to God's salvific plan for men and women. The friendships that Aquilina highlights, through his accessible prose and prudent inclusion of patristic excerpts, show the reader that Christ has come into the world to redeem friendship. And indeed, as Aquilina presents in this volume, friendship often requires more than a bit of redemption. *Friendship and the Fathers* is not a romanticized account of friendship. Even the saints fought. And yet through it all, they bestow to us an icon of what friendship in Christ means. This work of friendship, as Aquilina argues, is integral to evangelization in our age."

TIM O'MALLEY

Director of Online Education, McGrath Institute for Church Life, Notre Dame University

"The secret of the early Church's phenomenal growth was friendship. Mike Aquilina, through the words and friendships of the Fathers, unfolds anew for us the elements of this lost art of loving. It may be lost in our age, but it is essential for the regrowth of the modern Church because it is in friendships that strangers most frequently meet Christ."

PATRICK FAGAN
Director of the Marriage and Religion Research Initiative,
Catholic University of America

"This is a timely book for the Church in our present age. It is as rich and deep as it is plain and simple. Aquilina contrasts the early rapid spread of Christianity with our own apparently meeker contributions to evangelization. He introduces key Church Fathers and discovers that their secret to evangelization was authentic friendship; simply befriending family, neighbors, coworkers, and even strangers. He proposes the early Christian practice of friendship holds the key to our present need to evangelize and re-evangelize the world. Entertaining, insightful, and witty, this book promises to help start a new Christian revolution, a revolution of friendship, by immersing ourselves in the world of our earliest Christian brothers and sisters, so that we might be inspired to immerse ourselves in the lives of our family, friends, and neighbors today. I cannot recommend this book highly enough."

JEFFREY MORROW
Professor of Theology, Seton Hall University

"A wonderful collection of the wisdom of the Fathers on friendship—judiciously chosen texts and helpful commentary. Mike Aquilina has shown us that the Fathers can be our friends because they can relate to us and lead us to friendship with God. This volume will both console and challenge."

STEPHEN HILDEBRAND
Professor of Theology, Franciscan University

FRIENDSHIP
and the FATHERS

FRIENDSHIP
and the FATHERS

HOW THE EARLY
CHURCH EVANGELIZED

❧ MIKE AQUILINA ❧

EMMAUS
ROAD
PUBLISHING

Steubenville, Ohio
www.emmausroad.org

Emmaus Road Publishing
1468 Parkview Circle
Steubenville, Ohio 43952
©2021 Mike Aquilina
All rights reserved. Published 2021
Printed in the United States of America

Library of Congress Control Number 2021934995
ISBN: 978-1-64585-112-7 hardcover /
978-1-64585-113-4 paperback / 978-1-64585-114-1 ebook

Cover design and layout by Emily Demary
Cover image: *Heilige Basilius en de heilige Gregorius van Nazianze* (1666/1707), Gerard Edelinck, Rijksmuseum, Amsterdam, Netherlands

For Antonio

A friend is more to be longed for than the light. . . . A friend is sweeter than the present life.

—St. John Chrysostom

ACKNOWLEDGMENTS

THIS BOOK is the product of many friendships.

Credit for the idea goes to Dr. Patrick Fagan of The Catholic University of America. I was returning to my seat after presenting a paper, when Pat stopped me and whispered: "You should write a book about the Fathers and friendship." I replied: "There's not enough material." Then I sat down and, going from memory, I started making a list. Back in my hotel that night, I expanded the list. When I got home to my library, I found still more material. Before a week was up, I had a superabundance of material and wondered how I could ever reduce it to just one book. Before two weeks were up, I had submitted a proposal.

My friend of thirty years, Christopher Bailey, helped me immeasurably by producing translations of some ancient texts that have never appeared in English. All translations marked as new are his.

Other friends were benefactors in other ways. Kevin Knight (webmaster at NewAdvent.org) and Roger Pearse (Tertullian.org) generously allowed me to use and adapt their e-texts for this book. Both men's websites include libraries of translations of the Fathers. In this book I've drawn especially from the e-texts of three series that were first published in the nineteenth century: the *Ante-Nicene Fathers* (ANF) and the *Nicene and Post-Nicene Fathers* (NPNF1 and NPNF2). I have taken the liberty of modernizing some English translations to make them more accessible to today's readers.

I have been associated with Emmaus Road Press since its founding. I count as friends all the people there who worked on this book, but especially Chris Erickson, Scott Hahn, Rob Corzine, Alicia Boyle, and Katie Takats.

My wife, Terri, is my dearest friend and inspires all the work I do.

In the last place (as all too often), I'll acknowledge the very Friend who effected the revolution in friendship (John 15:15).

CONTENTS

INTRODUCTION

WE CAN BE FORGIVEN, we moderns, for any jealousy we feel toward the early Christians. In his 1996 study, *The Rise of Christianity*, the sociologist Rodney Stark attempted to quantify the growth of the Church through the first three centuries of Christian history—centuries of intermittent persecution, when the practice of the faith was a capital crime. His startling conclusion was that the Church grew throughout this period at a steady rate of forty percent per decade, and that most of the growth took place in big cities, where population is densest.

Critics piled on. Those numbers just couldn't be true—even though they seemed to be. Stark answered his critics definitively in his 2007 follow-up study, *Cities of God*.

In 2017 the historian Thomas A. Robinson argued that the problem with Stark's thesis was not that the numbers were too high, but that Stark did not go far enough. Whereas Stark described Christianity as mostly an urban phenomenon, Robinson saw abundant evidence for Church growth in the far reaches of rural areas. In other words, from its earliest years, Christianity spread everywhere.

The numbers can be simultaneously encouraging and dispiriting to Christians living two millennia after the fact. They're encouraging because they prove the universal appeal of the Gospel. They're dispiriting because the Church is not

1

coming close to those numbers today. Not only are we not in the ballpark; we're not even in the parking lot.

In spite of religious freedom—in spite of our wealth—in spite of a proliferation of institutional apostolates—we're not converting the world the way we did when we were poor and persecuted.

Stark and Robinson both suggest reasons for the early Church's phenomenal success. The former emphasizes the Christian response in times of crisis, such as pandemics. He also speaks of the enhanced status of women in Christian society. Robinson proposes that there was a compounding of crises—disease, war, earthquakes, famines—that made people more open to the Gospel.

The common narrative, however, is a story of friendship. There was, as far as we know, no talk of evangelistic methods or institutional programs in the underground Church. The evidence seems so simple as to be more incredible, at first sight, than Rodney Stark's hard-earned analytics.

As we move from the macro view to the micro—from the numbers to the paper trail—it seems that Christians converted the world simply by befriending their next-door neighbors and persevering in friendship.

"But when one of the parties is very far separated, as a god is from human beings, friendship cannot exist," said the Greek philosopher Aristotle, four hundred years before Christ.

"I have called you friends," said God incarnate (John 15:15).

That, in a word, is the Christian revolution. I propose that it is a revolution whose time has come again, for we've reached a convergence of crises that resemble the cluster of cataclysms the world saw in the third century. But the principal crisis is the disappearance of friendship.

Sociologists at the University of Arizona and Duke University conducted a longitudinal study on social isolation from 1985 to 2005. In 1985 they found that most Americans could name three people they considered very close friends and confidants. By 2005, however, one in four Americans reported having no close friends—no one in whom they could discuss their thoughts or struggles. The number of the self-identified friendless had doubled in twenty years.[1]

This is a crisis because it affects us not only mentally but physically as well. And it's not just op-ed writers and psychologists with an axe to grind who worry about loneliness. In 2018 the British government announced that it was going to treat loneliness as a public-health crisis. Most of the country's general practitioners saw at least one patient a day whose big problem was loneliness, "which is linked to a range of damaging health impacts, like heart disease, strokes and Alzheimer's disease."

The government actually appointed a Minister for Loneliness to coordinate the response to this crisis. With new funding and organization, doctors will be able to prescribe human interaction. They'll be able to refer patients to a network of community services that can get people together to do something fun.

It almost sounds like a Monty Python sketch. Is it really the government's job to make friends for us?

---

[1] Miller McPherson et al., "Social Isolation in America: Changes in Core Discussion Networks over Two Decades," *American Sociological Review* (June 2006): 353–375.

But the problem may be so big that nothing else can make a dent in it. It's "one of the greatest public health challenges of our time," Prime Minister Theresa May said when she introduced the government's Loneliness Strategy.[2] She cited depressing statistics about how many elderly people go for more than a month at a time without talking to a single friend or family member. Loneliness—and presumably what to do about it—will even be part of the curriculum in primary and secondary schools.[3]

But why are we so lonely?

We're more connected, and to more people, than at any other time in history. But we don't feel connected at all. You've probably heard the complaints. They sound like jokes, but you can hear the despair behind them. "I have 427 friends on Facebook! Why am I so lonely?"

We're connected to everyone, and we feel all alone.

Part of that is because social media has trivialized the meaning of "friend." You may have 427 friends on Facebook. But how many of those 427 would come to your funeral?

A "friend," by social media's definition, is someone whose random thoughts appear in your feed.

And that leads us to the much bigger and more insidious problem.

———

"Friendship may be shortly defined: *a perfect conformity of*

---

[2] Press release: "PM Launches Government's First Loneliness Strategy," October 15, 2018, https://www.gov.uk/government/news/pm-launches-governments-first-loneliness-strategy.

[3] Policy Paper: Loneliness Annual Report January 2020, https://www.gov.uk/government/publications/loneliness-annual-report-the-first-year/loneliness-annual-report-january-2020--2.

opinions upon all religious and civil subjects, united with the highest degree of mutual esteem and affection," says Cicero,[4] a pagan Roman of the first century before Christ.

Cicero's definition seems reasonable and considered. And yet one of the longest pieces in this book is going to reject it explicitly. In the delightful *Octavius* by Minucius Felix, you'll meet two Christians and their pagan friend, at a time when Christianity was illegal and technically punishable by death.

Certainly two Christians can't agree with a pagan on religious matters. And as for civil matters, the pagan thinks the laws against Christianity are reasonable and good for the empire.

Can two Christians possibly be friends with a pagan when he thinks their religion ought to be wiped out of the empire? Cicero would laugh at the very idea. But the *Octavius* was written to show exactly what can happen when Christians and pagans are friends. Spoiler alert: the pagan becomes a Christian.

Does that sound farfetched? The evidence—from former pagans' conversion stories—shows that it was a common outcome. Christianity certainly didn't have force on its side, and Christians couldn't rent halls and have big revival meetings to convert the heathens. The only thing they had going for them was an *apostolate of friendship*. Christians made friends, and then they made their friends Christians.

But that depended on making friends who were *different*. It depended on accepting that friends could be imperfect.

It depended on rejecting Cicero's definition.

Cicero would have loved Facebook.

---

[4] Cicero, *Laelius 20,* as translated by Melmoth, 33.

Social media picks up Cicero's definition of friendship and runs with it. Facebook and the others thrive by giving you more of what you already think, more to agree with, more to be outraged by. They create a virtual world where all sane people think the way you do and everyone who thinks differently is beyond the pale. They shrink our big, complicated world into a perfect little marble. It's just what we always wanted.

And it's lonely.

In the real world, friendships don't work that way. In the real world, our friends surprise us. We find people who believe the same things we do, but we also find people who believe wildly different things. We become friends for reasons we can't explain. Cicero would be appalled. We're so irrational!

But if God—who has no equal—has befriended us, who are we to place *anyone* outside the reach of our friendship? If Christianity is a participation in divine life, then grace makes us omni-capable in friendship. We can be friends with the most unlikely people.

That's our job, in fact. Tax collectors and sinners—those were the people Jesus hung out with. "Doesn't he know what kind of woman that is?" people whispered behind his back. But Jesus found his friends in the most unlikely places. He didn't make friends with people who were like him. He made friends with people who were different—the people who needed him most.

Jesus declares his Apostles to be friends—all of them sinners, and one of them even a tax collector. He also declares, repeatedly, that we must do the things he does. He establishes a pattern of evangelism that the Fathers followed. They made unlikely friends, too. Some of them made pagan friends and converted them. And some of them were pagans who made Christian friends and were converted.

That's the Christian pattern of friendship. It starts with the Incarnation. The central event of history is the ultimate act of friendship.

———

In the beginning, the Bible tells us, human beings walked and talked with God as a friend. It's one of the bitter ironies of the story, though, that we don't get a full picture of that relationship until it's gone terribly wrong.

> And they heard the sound of the LORD God walking in the garden in the cool of the day, and the man and his wife hid themselves from the presence of the LORD God among the trees of the garden. (Gen 3:8)

It's clear from the way the story is told that it's perfectly normal for the Lord to come strolling in the garden, and what's *not* normal is that the man and the woman hide from him.

The story in Genesis uses "figurative language," as the Catechism of the Catholic Church calls it (390), to show us the true state of our relationship with God. It's broken. We could have been God's friend, but when we follow our own way—as Adam and Eve did—we can't have that kind of friendship with God. Yet that's the friendship God really wants to have with us.

We see glimpses of it later in the Old Testament. Extraordinary individuals came close to the ideal. Abraham "was called the friend of God" (Jas 2:23). He was confident enough to haggle with God over the destruction of Sodom, talking him down from fifty righteous inhabitants to ten (see Gen 18:20–33). Exodus tells us that "the LORD used to speak to Moses face to face, as a man speaks to his friend" (Exod 33:11).

But most people couldn't have that relationship with God. The gap between our sin and God's holiness was so great that his holiness would literally burn us up—which is exactly what happened to the sons of Aaron.

> Now Nadab and Abihu, the sons of Aaron, each took his censer, and put fire in it, and laid incense on it, and offered unholy fire before the LORD, such as he had not commanded them. And fire came forth from the presence of the LORD and devoured them, and they died before the LORD. (Lev 10:1–2)

This was what happened if you tried to do things your own way.

The only thing that could bridge that gap was the Incarnation. Since we could never make ourselves equal to God, God had to come down to our level.

Once that had happened, there was no more chasm between us and God.

And if we could be friends with God, then we could certainly be friends with *anybody*.

However, we shouldn't dismiss the concerns of Aristotle and Cicero. Inequality can introduce complications and patterns of codependency into a relationship. That's very, very real, and the ancients' observations of this are remarkable. Some of the Church Fathers will tell us, right here in this book, that a friendship is doomed unless the friends are both virtuous.

But Christ taught us that our life has a direction. We're all sinners, and we're all headed for heaven—if we're willing to go. So instead of despairing over our imperfect friendships, the Fathers tell us how to improve in virtue, so our friendships can improve as well. And as Irenaeus will tell us, it's all possible because God himself elevated us from servants to friends.

———

As we go from the very early Christian era to late antiquity, we see two distinct stages in the Fathers' writings on friendship.

The first stage is what we might call the pre-Constantine stage. When Christianity was an illegal underground movement, it spread from friend to friend. That was the only way it could spread. And anyone who became a Christian was making a big sacrifice just by that very identity. You could die in one of the periodic persecutions. But even if you didn't get thrown to the beasts—and obviously most Christians didn't—you still had to be watchful all the time. It was a pagan world out there, and everything conspired to pull Christians away from their straight and narrow path back to the easy road.

So the Fathers of that time seem most concerned with the idea of extending God's friendship to the world. Because God himself called us friends, we have a duty to bring more and more of God's people into our circle of friends. John the Apostle even used the term "the friends" to describe the Christian community: "The friends greet you. Greet the friends, every one of them" (3 John 15).

After Constantine things changed drastically. Christianity was no longer illegal—in fact, it was the favored religion of the Empire, and after a few more generations, the official religion of the Empire. So Christians no longer had to watch their backs just because they were Christian. Being Christian was the default choice. If you really didn't care about religion or virtue, you called yourself Christian.

With that change, we start to see the Fathers concerning themselves more with the effect of bad company on good morals. They put more emphasis on the dangers of the wrong *kind* of friendship. That's because now, when most of the people around you were nominally Christian, a lot of people were the wrong *kind* of Christian. One of the memorable sins St. Augustine brings up in his *Confessions* is the time when he stole some pears from a tree—a crime he attributes to the bad influence of his friends.[5] He didn't want the pears: he just wanted to be one of the guys.

Still, no one ever wrote more touchingly on the need for friends than Augustine did. And few of the Fathers seem to have felt that need more strongly. If he was worried about the possibility of bad influences among friends, he was much more appalled by the idea of a life without friends at all.

Thanks to his *Confessions,* Augustine never has to worry about that possibility. Everyone who reads that book becomes Augustine's friend for life. And you'll make many other friends in this book. Across the centuries, their vivid personalities come to life. There's Minucius Felix, the urbane lawyer who loves a stroll on the beach. There's Jerome, the famous grump with a weakness for colorful insults. There's the inflexible Basil of Caesarea and the all-too-flexible Gregory Nazianzen. Once you know them, you'll want to invite them back often for a visit. They can be our friends,

---

[5] Augustine, *Confessions* 2.9.17.

too. Augustine, after all, gained a close friend in Paulinus of Nola, even though the two never met. He only knew Paulinus through his writing—as Paulinus knew him.

And while the Fathers work their way into our hearts, perhaps they can begin to teach us the cure for our loneliness. After all, the problems of our day are not too different from the problems of their day. Their lives were busy. They lived in an uncertain world of big cities, massive bureaucracies, and constant change. They had big problems. But they found the time for friendship.

No—we shouldn't say they found the time. They *made* the time. There is one thing all the Fathers agree on: friendship takes work. It's a warning to us: we can't be lazy and expect to have friends. But it's also a message of hope. With God's grace giving us the power of friendship, we *can* overcome our loneliness. We can be the friends we ought to be and have the friends we want to have. And we can do it because God himself has called us friends.

1.

IRENAEUS

St. Irenaeus of Lyons was a Greek from the East who ended up way out west in Gaul—today's France—as bishop of Lyons in the late AD 100s. Christianity was still an illegal cult and would be for more than a century. Persecutions sometimes flared up, but long intervals of peace allowed the Church to grow.

Aside from the persecutions, the biggest worry Irenaeus had was the multiplication of heretical sects—groups that called themselves Christian but believed all kinds of things that Jesus never taught. In Lyons the largest of these was the Gnostics, which was actually a squirming viper-pit of different Gnostic sects constantly giving birth to more Gnostic sects. It was almost impossible to sort out what they all believed. It took Irenaeus a whole book to do it.

In *Against Heresies,* Irenaeus patiently described what each of the splinter groups of Gnostics believed, and why it was contrary to what Jesus and the Apostles had taught. One of the persistent Gnostic ideas was that the God of the Old Testament was a different being from the God of the New Testament. The Old Testament God was the evil creator of this world in Gnostic theology, and Christ came to free us from bondage to that creator. Irenaeus spends a lot of time explaining why the Old Testament God is still our God, and as part of that explanation he has to account for the change in our relationship with God that happened when Christ came.

The difference is not that we have a new God now, he says. The difference is that now God is our friend. When the Word of God came to us, he gave us all the power necessary to be friends of God, like Abraham. And when God is your friend, you have immortal life.

But this is our Lord, the Word of God. At first he certainly did draw slaves to God. But afterwards he set those free who were subject to him, as he himself tells his disciples: "No longer do I call you servants, for the servant does not know what his master is doing; but I have called you friends, for all that I have heard from my Father I have made known to you" (John 15:15).

Here, where he says, "No longer do I call you servants," he indicates in the clearest possible way that he himself was the one who originally appointed for men that bondage with respect to God through the law, and then afterwards gave them freedom. And when he says, "for the servant does not know what his master is doing," he points out, by means of his own advent, the ignorance of a people in a servile condition.

But when he calls his disciples the friends of God, he plainly declares himself to be the Word of God, whom Abraham also followed voluntarily and without chains, because of the noble nature of his faith, and so became the friend of God (see Jas 2:23). But the Word of God did not accept the friendship of Abraham as though he *needed* it, for he was perfect from the beginning: "before Abraham was," he says, "I am" (John 8:58). No, he accepted it so that he in his goodness might bestow eternal life upon Abraham himself, since the friendship of God imparts immortality to those who embrace it.

—Irenaeus, *Against Heresies* 4.13

2.

MINUCIUS FELIX

Two Christians and a pagan go to the beach. Three Christians come back.

That's the simple premise behind *Octavius,* a dialogue written at some time around the year 200 by Marcus Minucius Felix. This was a time when Christianity was still illegal, and the penalty was death. Nevertheless, Christians were everywhere. Pagans had heard terrible stories about what Christians did at their secret meetings. But more and more of those pagans were finding out the truth and turning Christian.

That was what had happened to Minucius Felix and his friend Octavius.

During his time, Minucius Felix was one of the great prose stylists of his time. Scholars of Latin literature make that judgment confidently, even though this is the only one of his works that has survived. It's more than brilliant enough to carry a literary reputation through millennia.

Minucius Felix was a lawyer from North Africa but living and practicing law in the empire's capital. It's clear that he had a superb education. He wrote Latin with the style and verve of Cicero and Seneca. His *Octavius* is a work of dramatic fiction.

"Fiction" doesn't mean purely imaginary. Indeed it's likely that all three of its main characters were real people, and that the dialogue was reconstructed from the author's vivid memory of a real event. The names of all three characters have turned up in civic inscriptions from this period—all found in North Africa, and all from the period in which the *Octavius* is set.

The author himself, Minucius Felix, was a notable public figure in his day, and his reputation survived him by at least a couple centuries. He was at the top of his profession, practicing law in the city whose laws governed the earth. He was a Christian, but that had not impeded his career. The anti-Christian laws were on the books, and Christianity was technically a capital crime, but Minucius Felix seems to have lived during a lull between active persecutions.

This happened intermittently. The emperors despised the Christians for their superstition, and popular opinion often favored active persecution. But with every decade the Christians grew more numerous, and so they included an increasing number of people considered indispensable. In times of war, for example, the Empire came to depend upon Christian soldiers, because Christian soldiers were reliably courageous. In times of epidemic, the major cities came to depend upon Christian doctors for the same reason.

Minucius Felix was probably one of those indispensable men. His gifts were certainly extraordinary—and clearly high among his gifts was friendship. He surely had many friends in high places.

His two companions in the *Octavius* were also very important citizens. They were the kind, after all, who got their names carved into cornerstones that survive for millennia. Like Minucius Felix, they were public figures.

Technically the literary form of the drama is a dialogue. It's like the sparkling philosophical dramas of Plato and Cicero. It's a story of friends having a conversation and disagreeing vehemently and frankly, as only friends can, and needing to come to a resolution, as only friends can.

The structure of the dialogue is very simple. There's an opening section that sets up the debate. Minucius' pagan friend, Caecilius Natalis, is offended by something his Christian friend, Octavius Januarius, said, so they decide that each will lay out his best arguments. Minucius himself is chosen as judge. The pagan gives his arguments against Christianity; then Octavius refutes them very effectively—so effectively that Minucius doesn't have to do any judging.

But *Octavius* is more than an argument for Christianity. It's a meditation on friendship—and Christian friendship in particular. What does it mean for a Christian to have a non-Christian friend? Is it a problem or an opportunity?

Minucius Felix writes as a former unbeliever. Both he and Octavius had been ardent opponents of Christianity in their youth. Both had participated directly in the interrogation and condemnation of Christians. Both had attempted to drive Christians to deny the faith.

Yet his own backstory made him love his nonbelieving friends all the more. He knew firsthand that conversion was possible, even in the hard cases. And that reasoned discussion, in the context of friendship, was a good beginning to any conversion story.

So he put that conversation into beautiful writing. He placed it in the most beautiful setting he knew. And he gave a sympathetic voice to the concerns of his most hostile opponents. He wanted to make them friends, and he wanted to make them Christians.

This dialogue is almost as notable for its charming setting as for its argument. After all these centuries, we nearly forget that the ancient Christians were human beings. They loved to feel the breeze on a fine autumn day. They liked to go to the beach and feel the sand between their toes. They loved to skip shells across the water and see whose shell could go farthest.

The *Octavius* is the only Christian document of its time that reminds us of all these beautiful things. At the charming beach resort and seaport of Ostia, you can have an earnest debate and a day at the shore all in one.

When I think about what I remember of Octavius, my excellent and most faithful companion, the sweetness and charm of the man clings to me so much that it almost seems as if I were going back into the past, and not merely recalling things that have long since happened and gone by. Thus, the longer it has been since I could actually see him, the more the thought of him is bound up in my heart and in my most intimate feelings.

And it was not without reason that that remarkable and holy man, when he departed this life, left me an unbounded regret for him—especially since he himself also glowed with such a love for me at all times, that, whether in matters of amusement or of business, he agreed with me in similarity of will, in either liking or disliking the same things. You would think that one mind had been shared between us two. Thus he alone was my confidant in my loves, my companion in my mistakes; and when, after the gloom had been dispersed, I emerged from the abyss of darkness into the light of wisdom and truth, he did not cast off his associate, but—what is more glorious still—he outstripped him.

And thus, when my thoughts were traversing the entire period of our intimacy and friendship, my mind fixed itself chiefly on that time when by very weighty arguments he converted Caecilius, who was still sticking to his superstitious vanities, to the true religion.

A DAY AT THE BEACH

Octavius had hurried to Rome on business, and also to visit me, having left his home, his wife, his children, and that which is most attractive in children, while yet their innocent years are attempting only half-uttered words—a language all the sweeter for the very imperfection of the faltering tongue. When he arrived, I cannot express in words with how great and with how impatient a joy I exulted, since the unexpected presence of a man so very dear to me greatly enhanced my gladness.

Therefore, after one or two days, when the frequent enjoyment of our continual association had satisfied the craving of affection, and when we had ascertained by mutual narrative all that we were ignorant of about one another by reason of our separation, we agreed to go to that very pleasant city Ostia, that my body might have a soothing and appropriate remedy for drying its humors from the marine bathing—especially as the holidays of the courts at the vintage-time had released me from my cares. For at that time, after the summer days, the autumn season was tending to a milder temperature.

It was early morning; we were going towards the sea along the riverbank, so that the gentle breezes might refresh our limbs, and the yielding sand might sink down under our easy footsteps with excessive pleasure—when Caecilius, seeing an image of Serapis, raised his hand to his mouth, as is the custom of the superstitious common people, and pressed a kiss on it with his lips.

Then Octavius said, "It is not fitting for a good man, my brother Marcus, to leave a man who stays by your side at home and abroad in this blindness of vulgar ignorance. You let him give himself up to stones in broad daylight—however they may be carved into images, anointed and crowned. Now, you know that this error of his is as disgraceful to you as it is to him."

He was talking this way as we passed over the distance between the city and the sea, and we were now walking on the broad and open shore. There the gently rippling wave was smoothing the outside sands as if it would level them for a promenade; and as the sea is always restless, even when the winds are lulled, it came up on the shore, although not with waves crested and foaming, yet with waves crisped and curling. Just then we were excessively delighted at its vagaries, as on the very threshold of the water we were wetting the soles of our feet, and it now by turns approaching broke upon our feet, and now the wave retiring and retracing its course, sucked itself back into itself.

And thus, slowly and quietly going along, we tracked the coast of the gently bending shore, beguiling the way with stories. These stories were related by Octavius, who was talking about navigation.

But when we had occupied a sufficiently reasonable time of our walk with discourse, we came back the same way, retracing our steps. And when we came to that place where the little ships, drawn up on an oaken framework, were lying at rest supported out of the way of ground-rot, we saw some boys eagerly gesticulating as they played at skipping shells into the sea. This is how they play the game: they choose a shell from the shore, rubbed and made smooth by the tossing of the waves; then they take hold of the shell in a horizontal position with the fingers and send it flying as low down as possible on the waves, so that when thrown it may either skim the back of the wave, or may swim as it glides along with a smooth impulse, or may spring up as it cleaves the top of the waves, and rise as if lifted up with repeated springs. The boy whose shell both went out furthest and leaped up most frequently was the winner.

Caecilius challenges Octavius to a debate

But while we were all enjoying this spectacle, Caecilius was paying no attention, not laughing at the contest. He was silent, uneasy, and standing apart, and we could tell by his face that something was worrying him.

So I said to him, "What's the matter? What's happened to your usual liveliness, Caecilius? Where's that joy we usually see in your glances even in serious matters?"

"For some time," he said, "our friend Octavius' speech

has bitterly vexed and worried me. He attacked you and reproached you with negligence, but what he meant to do, under cover of that charge, was more seriously condemn me for ignorance. So I will go on from there: the matter is now wholly and entirely between me and Octavius. If he is willing that I, a man of that form of opinion, should argue with him, he will now at once perceive that it is easier to hold an argument among his comrades, than to engage in close conflict after the manner of the philosophers. Let's sit down on those rocky jetties set up there to protect the baths, the ones that run far out into the deep, so that we may be able both to rest after our journey, and to argue with more attention."

And at his word we sat down, so that, by covering me on either side, they sheltered me in the midst of the three. Nor was this a matter of observance, or of rank, or of honor, because friendship always either receives or makes equals. No, it was simply so that, as an arbitrator, and being near to both, I might give my attention, and being in the middle, I might separate the two.

Then Caecilius began thus:

CAECILIUS RECOMMENDS SKEPTICISM

You, Marcus my brother, have no doubts about the subject under discussion, since, being carefully informed in both kinds of life, you have rejected the one and assented to the other. Yet in the present case you must make your mind up to hold the balance of a very fair judge, not leaning on one side—otherwise your decision might seem not to arise so much from our arguments as from your own perceptions.

So if you sit in judgment on me, as a person who is new, and as one ignorant of either side, there is no difficulty in making plain that all things in human affairs are doubtful, uncertain, and unsettled, and that all things are rather probable than true. Thus it is less surprising that some, from the weariness of thoroughly investigating truth, should rashly succumb to any sort of opinion rather than persevere in exploring it with persistent diligence.

And thus everyone must be indignant, everyone must feel pain, that certain persons—and these unskilled in learning, strangers to literature, without knowledge even of sordid arts—should dare to determine on any certainty concerning the nature at large, and the divine majesty, when there have been so many sects in every age, and philosophy itself is still deliberating. And not without reason: our intelligence is so far below what it would take to understand the divine, that neither is it given us to know, nor is it permitted to search, nor is it religious to try to take, the things that are supported in suspense in the heaven above us, or the things which are deeply submerged below the earth. We may rightly seem happy and prudent enough if, according to that ancient oracle of the sage, we should know ourselves intimately. . . .

Caecilius argues that either the universe and human beings are things that just happened randomly, or there is some design that we will never be able to understand. Since we don't know, it's better to worship the traditional gods.

This is why we see in all empires, and provinces, and cities, that each nation has its national rites of worship, and adores its local gods. The Eleusinians worship Ceres; the Phrygians worship Mater; the Epidaurians worship Aesculapius; the Chaldaeans worship Belus; the Syrians worship Astarte; the Taurians worship Diana; the Gauls worship Mercurius.

And the Romans worship all divinities. This is why their power and authority has occupied the circuit of the whole world: this is why their empire has reached beyond the paths of the sun, and the bounds of the ocean itself: because in their arms they practice a religious valor; because they fortify their city with the religions of sacred rites, with chaste virgins, with many honors, and the names of priests; because, when besieged and taken, all but the Capitol alone, they worship the gods whom any other people would have despised when they were angry; and through the lines of the Gauls, marveling at the audacity of their superstition, they move unarmed with weapons, but armed with the worship of their religion.[1] In the city of an enemy, when taken while still in the fury of victory, they venerate the conquered deities. In all directions they seek for the gods of the strangers and make them their own; while they build altars even to unknown divinities, and to the Manes.

Thus, by acknowledging the sacred institutions of all nations, they have also deserved their dominion.

---

[1] In 390 BC, the Gauls invaded Rome, and for a while only the Capitoline Hill was under the control of the Roman soldiers.

When the Romans worship the gods and pay attention to the auguries, says Caecilius, they prosper. When they ignore the traditions, they fail.

WHO ARE THESE CHRISTIANS? THE DREGS OF SOCIETY.

Therefore, since the consent of all nations concerning the existence of the immortal gods remains established, although their nature or their origin remains uncertain, I will not allow anyone puffed up with such boldness, and with I know not what irreligious wisdom, to try to undermine or weaken this religion, so ancient, so useful, so wholesome. . . .

Having gathered together from the lowest dregs the more unskilled, and women!—women are gullible and easy to push around—they establish a herd of a profane conspiracy, which is bound together by nightly meetings, and solemn fasts and inhuman meats—not by any sacred rite, but by that which requires expiation. They are a people skulking and shunning the light, silent in public, but garrulous in corners. They despise the temples as dead-houses, they reject the gods, they laugh at sacred things; wretched, they pity, if they are allowed, the priests; half-naked themselves, they despise honors and purple robes. Oh, wondrous folly and incredible audacity! They despise present torments, although they fear those that are uncertain and future; and while they fear to die after death, they do not fear to die for the present: so does a deceitful hope soothe their fear with the consolation of a revival.

Horrible stories are told about their secret rites

And now, as wickeder things advance more fruitfully, and abandoned manners creep on day by day, those abominable shrines of an impious assembly are growing up throughout the whole world. Certainly this confederacy ought to be rooted out and execrated. They know one another by secret marks and insignia, and they love one another almost before they know one another. Everywhere also there is mingled among them a certain religion of lust, and they call one another promiscuously brothers and sisters, so that even ordinary debauchery may be made incestuous by that name: it is thus that their vain and senseless superstition glories in crimes.

And intelligent rumor would not speak of things so great and various, and demanding to be apologized for in advance, unless truth were at the bottom of it. I hear that they adore the head of an ass, that basest of creatures, consecrated by I know not what silly persuasion—a worthy and appropriate religion for such manners. Some say that they worship the genitals of their pontiff and priest, and adore the nature, so to speak, of their common parent. I do not know whether these things are false. Certainly secret and nocturnal rites deserve some suspicion; and he who explains their ceremonies by reference to a man punished by extreme suffering for his wickedness, and to the deadly wood of the cross, appropriates fitting altars for reprobate and wicked men, that they may worship what they deserve.

Now the story about the initiation of young novices is as detestable as it is well known. An infant covered over with flour, in order to deceive the unwary, is placed before him who is to be stained with their rites: this infant is slain by the young pupil, who has been urged on as if to harmless blows on the surface of the meal, with dark and secret wounds. Thirstily—O horror!—they lick up its blood; eagerly they divide its limbs. By this victim they are pledged together; with this consciousness of wickedness they are covenanted to mutual silence. Such sacred rites as these are more foul than any sacrileges.

And their banqueting is well known—everyone talks about it. Even the speech of our Cirtensian[2] testifies to it. On a solemn day they assemble at the feast, with all their children, sisters, mothers, people of every sex and of every age. There, after much feasting, when the fellowship has grown warm, and the fervor of incestuous lust has grown hot with drunkenness, a dog that has been tied to the chandelier is provoked, by throwing a small piece of offal beyond the length of a line by which he is bound, to rush and spring; and thus the conscious light being overturned and extinguished in the shameless darkness, the connections of abominable lust involve them in the uncertainty of fate. Although they are not all actually incestuous, they are certainly all incestuous in their hearts, since they all desire it.

---

[2] Marcus Cornelius Fronto, tutor of the emperor Marcus Aurelius. It may not be a coincidence that Marcus Aurelius, famous for his wisdom, was also a notorious persecutor of the Christians.

Christians believe in an absurd God

I purposely pass over many things, for those that I have mentioned are already too many. And the obscurity of their vile religion is enough to tell us that all these things are true, or most of them. Why else would they take such pains to conceal and to cloak whatever they worship? Honorable things always rejoice in publicity, while crimes are kept secret. Why have they no altars, no temples, no acknowledged images? Why do they never speak openly, never congregate freely? It must be because what they adore and conceal is either worthy of punishment, or something to be ashamed of.

And besides, where does he come from, or who is he, or where is he, this one God, solitary, desolate, whom no free people, no kingdoms, and not even Roman superstition, have known?

Christian ideas about God and the Resurrection are absurd, Caecilius insists. And not only is the Resurrection a crazy idea, but Christians miss the best parts of this life while they wait for a fantasy of a future life. We should imitate Socrates and confess our ignorance of things above our understanding.

In my opinion, too, things that are uncertain ought to be left as they are. Nor, while so many and so great men are deliberating, should we rashly and boldly give an opinion in another direction. Otherwise we might either bring in a childish superstition or overthrow all religion.

MINUCIUS WARNS CAECILIUS NOT TO BE CARRIED AWAY BY HIS OWN ELOQUENCE

So Caecilius concluded; and smiling cheerfully (for the vehemence of his prolonged discourse had relaxed the ardor of his indignation), he added, "And what does Octavius venture to reply to this, a man of the race of Plautus, who, while he was chief among the millers, was still the lowest of philosophers?"[3]

"Restrain your self-approval against him," I said; "for it is not worthy of you to exult at the harmony of your discourse before the subject has been more fully argued on both sides—especially since your reasoning is striving after truth, not praise."

Minucius suggests that it should be reason, not rhetoric, that prevails in this debate. With that instruction from the judge, Octavius begins.

[3] Plautus was a famous comic playwright—but not famous enough, according to one tradition, to keep him from having to turn a mill for a bakery.

31

OCTAVIUS INSISTS THAT THE ARGUMENT IS WHAT MATTERS, NOT THE CLASS OF THE SPEAKER

I will indeed speak as I am able to the best of my powers, and you must try along with me to dilute the very offensive strain of recriminations in the river of truthful words.

Nor will I disguise in the outset, that the opinion of my friend Natalis has swayed to and fro in such an erratic, vague, and slippery manner, that we are compelled to doubt whether your information was confused, or whether it wavered backwards and forwards by mere mistake. Sometimes he seemed to believe the gods; other times he was in a state of hesitation on the subject; so that the direct purpose of my reply was established with the greater uncertainty, by reason of the uncertainty of his proposition.

But in my friend Natalis I will not allow, I do not believe in, any chicanery. Far from his straightforwardness is crafty trickery!

Octavius suggests that Caecilius jumps between arguments because he is honestly confused about the truth, and so Octavius will clear it up for him. First, we should not be annoyed if even ignorant people speak rightly about the truth. All nature shows that there must be a God, says Octavius, giving many examples of elegant design in the world. And there must be one God, not many. Look at human history: did two kings ever manage to cooperate? Even the common people say, "God is great," indicating that they know there is one God. All the pagan philosophers agree that there is one God. Those ignorant Christians Caecilius complains about are saying the same things as the greatest philosophers of Athens!

The pagan myths are absurd and often disgusting

Read the writings of the Stoics,[4] or the writings of wise men: you will acknowledge these facts with me. . . . And you behold the swallow and the cymbal of Isis, and the tomb of your Serapis or Osiris empty, with his limbs scattered about.[5]

Then consider the sacred rites themselves, and their very mysteries: you will find mournful deaths, misfortunes, and funerals, and the griefs and wailings of the miserable gods. . . . Is it not ridiculous either to grieve for what you worship, or to worship that over which you grieve? Yet these were formerly Egyptian rites, and now are Roman ones. . . .

Cybele of Dindymus—I am ashamed to speak of it— could not entice her adulterous lover to lewdness. He unfortunately was pleasing to her, but she herself, the mother of many gods, was ugly and old. So she mutilated him, doubt-

---

[4] Because he seems to know so much about the Stoics and generally approves of them, many scholars believe that Minucius Felix was a Stoic before he became a Christian.

[5] In Egyptian mythology, Osiris (who was later amalgamated with Serapis) was murdered and cut in pieces by his brother, but his wife Isis collected the pieces and put them back together.

less so that she might make a god of the eunuch. On account of this story, the Galli also worship her by the punishment of their emasculated body.[6]

Now certainly these things are not sacred rites, but tortures. . . .

These fables and errors we learn from ignorant parents, and—even worse—we elaborate them in our very studies and instructions, especially in the verses of the poets, who as much as possible have prejudiced the truth by their authority.

And for this reason, Plato rightly expelled from the state which he had founded in his discourse, the illustrious Homer whom he had praised and crowned. For he was the one especially who, in the Trojan wars, allowed your gods to interfere in the affairs and doings of men—even though he made jokes of them. He brought them together in contest; he wounded Venus; he bound, wounded, and drove away Mars. He relates that Jupiter was set free by Briareus, so as not to be bound fast by the rest of the gods; and that he bewailed in showers of blood his son Sarpedon, because he could not snatch him from death; and that, enticed by the girdle of Venus, he lay more eagerly with his wife Juno than he used to do with his adulterous loves.

Elsewhere Hercules threw out dung, and Apollo is feeding cattle for Admetus. Neptune, however, builds walls for Laomedon, and the unfortunate builder did not receive the wages for his work. Then Jupiter's thunderbolt is fabricated on the anvil with the arms of Aeneas, although there were heaven, and thunderbolts, and lightnings long before

---

[6] The Galli were priests of Cybele. They became her priests by mutilating themselves during the frenzied festival of the goddess.

Jupiter was born in Crete; and neither could the Cyclops imitate, nor Jupiter himself help fearing, the flames of the real thunderbolt. Why should I speak of the detected adultery of Mars and Venus, and of the violence of Jupiter against Ganymede—a deed consecrated (as you say) in heaven?

And all these things have been put forward with this view, that a certain authority might be gained for the vices of men. By these fictions, and others like them, and by lies of a more attractive kind, the minds of boys are corrupted; and with the same fables clinging to them, they grow up even to the strength of mature age; and, poor wretches, they grow old in the same beliefs, although the truth is plain, if they will only seek after it.

All the best pagan writers agree that the legendary gods were originally human beings, Octavius says; in this, too, the Christians have the best philosophers on their side.

The worship of the pagan gods is full of absurdities

How much more truly do dumb animals naturally judge concerning your gods! Mice, swallows, kites, know that they have no feeling: they gnaw them, they trample on them, they sit on them; and unless you drive them off, they build their nests in the very mouth of your god. Spiders weave their webs over his face and suspend their threads from his very head. You wipe, clean, scrape, and you protect and fear those whom you make; while not one of you thinks that he ought to know God before he worships him. No, instead you desire without thinking about it to obey your ancestors, choosing rather to become an addition to the error of others, than to trust yourselves; in that you know nothing of what you fear. Thus avarice has been consecrated in gold and silver; thus the form of empty statues has been established; thus has arisen Roman superstition.

And if you reconsider the rites of these gods, how many things are laughable, and how many also pitiable! Naked people run about in the raw winter; some walk with hats, and carry around old bucklers, or beat drums, or lead their gods begging through the streets. Some sacred sites it is permitted to approach once a year, some it is forbidden to visit at all. There is one place where a man may not go, and there are some that are sacred from women: it is a crime needing atonement for a slave even to be present at some ceremonies. Some sacred places are crowned by a woman having one husband, some by a woman with many; and she who can reckon up most adulteries is sought after with most religious zeal.

Don't you think a man who makes libations of his own blood, and supplicates his god by his own wounds, would be better off if he were completely profane, than religious in such a way as this? And he whose shameful parts are cut off, how greatly does he wrong God in seeking to propitiate him in this manner! If God wanted eunuchs, he could bring them as such into existence, and would not make them so afterwards.

Who does not perceive that people of unsound mind, and of weak and degraded apprehension, are foolish in these things, and that the very multitude of those who err affords to each of them mutual patronage? The only defense of the general madness is that there are so many mad people.

Rome prevailed by crime and cruelty, not piety

Nevertheless, you will say that that very superstition itself gave, increased, and established their empire for the Romans, since they prevailed not so much by their valor as by their religion and piety.

Doubtless the illustrious and noble justice of the Romans had its beginning from the very cradle of the growing empire. Did they not in their origin, when gathered together and fortified by crime, grow by the terror of their own fierceness? For the first people were assembled together as to an asylum. Abandoned people, profligate, incestuous, assassins, traitors, had flocked together; and in order that Romulus himself, their commander and governor, might excel his people in guilt, he committed fratricide. These are the first auspices of the religious state!

By and by they carried off, violated, and ruined foreign virgins, already betrothed, already destined for husbands, and even some young women from their marriage vows—a thing unexampled—and then engaged in war with their parents, that is, with their fathers-in-law, and shed the blood of their kindred.[7] What more irreligious, what more audacious, what

---

[7] The "Rape of the Sabine Women" is one of the most famous foundation legends of Rome.

could be safer than the very confidence of crime?

Now, to drive their neighbors from the land, to over-throw the nearest cities, with their temples and altars, to drive them into captivity, to grow up by the losses of others and by their own crimes, is the course of training common to the rest of the kings and the latest leaders with Romulus. Thus, whatever the Romans hold, cultivate, possess, is the spoil of their audacity. All their temples are built from the spoils of violence, that is, from the ruins of cities, from the spoils of the gods, from the murders of priests. This is to insult and scorn, to yield to conquered religions, to adore them when captive, after having vanquished them. For to adore what you have taken by force, is to consecrate sacrilege, not divinities. As often, therefore, as the Romans triumphed, so often they were polluted; and as many trophies as they gained from the nations, so many spoils did they take from the gods.

Therefore the Romans were not so great because they were religious, but because they were sacrilegious with impunity. . . .

You can find just as many stories of the augurs being wrong, says Octavius. But even when they are right, it is probably because demons, who are devoted to our destruction, are leading us astray.

As for the horrible rumors about Christians, Octavius and Minucius used to believe them, too, and even persecuted Christians in the courts—while at the same time defending the worst criminals. But then they learned the truth.

The accusations against Christians are really true of pagans

But how unjust it is, to form a judgment on things unknown and unexamined, as you do! Believe us ourselves when we are penitent. For we used to be the same as you, and while we were still blind and obtuse, we thought the same things as you—namely, that the Christians worshiped monsters, devoured infants, mingled in incestuous banquets. And we did not perceive that such fables as these were always set afloat by such people, and were never either inquired into nor proved; and that in so long a time no one had appeared to expose the Christians to obtain not only pardon for their crime, but also favor for its discovery. We did not even see that it could not be evil because a Christian, when accused, neither blushed nor feared, and only repented that he had not been one before.

But when we undertook to defend and protect some sacrilegious and incestuous persons, and even parricides, we did not think that these Christians were to be heard at all. Sometimes even, when we affected to pity them, we were more cruelly violent against them, so as to torture them when they confessed, to make them recant so that they might not perish; making use of a perverse inquisition against them, not to bring out the truth, but to compel a falsehood. And if anyone, by reason of greater weakness, overcome with suffering, and conquered, should deny that he was a Christian, we showed favor to him, as if by forswearing that name he had at once atoned for all his deeds by that simple denial.

Do not you acknowledge that we felt and did the same as you feel and do?

But, if reason and not the instigation of a demon were to judge, they should rather have been pressed not to disavow themselves Christians, but to confess themselves guilty of incests, of abominations, of sacred rites polluted, of infants immolated. For with these and such as these stories, did those same demons fill up the ears of the ignorant against us, to the horror of their execration. Nor yet was it wonderful, since the common report of men, which is, always fed by the scattering of falsehoods, is wasted away when the truth is brought to light. Thus this is the business of demons, for by them false rumors are both sown and cherished. . . .

Anyone who makes up stories against us about our adoring the members of the priest is trying to transfer to us what is actually true of himself. Those members are perhaps sacred to the lewdness of those among whom the whole sex is prostituted in every member, among whom lewdness is called sophistication; who envy the license of whores, who do abominable things with men—and if even the wickedest gossips fail to describe them, it is because they are more bored with than ashamed of the lewdness.[8]

Abomination! They allow themselves to be subject to such evil deeds as no age is so effeminate as to be able to bear, and no slavery so cruel as to be compelled to endure! . . .

---

[8] This section was left untranslated by the Victorian translator. As a compromise, this new translation is toned down from the original, which is very graphic.

Christians would never hurt a child — but pagans would

And now I would like to meet anyone who says or believes that we are initiated by the slaughter and blood of an infant. Do you think it can be possible for so tender, so little a body to receive those fatal wounds; for anyone to shed, pour forth, and drain that new blood of a baby, and of a man scarcely come into existence? No one can believe this, except one who can dare to do it.

And I see that you sometimes expose your begotten children to wild beasts and to birds; other times you crush them when strangled with a miserable kind of death. There are some women who, by drinking medical preparations, extinguish the source of the future man in their very bowels, and thus commit a parricide before they bring forth.

And these things certainly come down from the teaching of your gods. For Saturn did not expose his children but devoured them. With reason were infants sacrificed to him by parents in some parts of Africa, caresses and kisses repressing their crying, so that a weeping victim might not be sacrificed. Moreover, among the Tauri of Pontus, and to the Egyptian Busiris, it was a sacred rite to immolate their guests, and for the Galli to slaughter to Mercury human, or rather inhuman, sacrifices. The Roman sacrificers buried living a Greek man and a Greek woman, a Gallic man and a Gallic woman; and to this day, Jupiter Latiaris is worshiped by them with murder; and, what is worthy of the son of Saturn, he is gorged with the blood of an evil and criminal man. I believe that he himself taught Catiline to conspire under a compact of blood, and Bellona to steep her sacred rites with a draught of human gore, and taught men to heal epilepsy with the blood of a man, that is, with a worse disease. They also are not unlike to him who devour the wild beasts from the arena, besmeared and stained with blood, or fattened with the limbs or the entrails of men.

To us it is not lawful either to see or to hear of homicide; and so much do we shrink from human blood, that we do not use the blood even of edible animals in our food.

Incest, too, is typical of pagans, says Octavius, and at the highest levels—think of Egyptian royalty. It is the Christians who prize modesty and chastity.

CHRISTIANS HAVE NO IMAGES OF GOD BECAUSE GOD IS INVISIBLE

But do you think that we conceal what we worship, if we do not have temples and altars? But what image of God shall I make, since, if you think rightly, man himself is the image of God? What temple shall I build to him, when this whole world fashioned by his work cannot receive him? And when I, a man, dwell far and wide, shall I shut up the might of so great majesty within one little building? Would it not be better that God should be dedicated in our mind, consecrated in our inmost heart? Shall I offer victims and sacrifices to the Lord, things he has produced for my use, throwing his own gift back at him? It is ungrateful when the victim fit for sacrifice is a good disposition, and a pure mind, and a sincere judgment.

God cannot be seen precisely because he is the power behind everything, just as a powerful wind can blow everything but cannot be seen itself. As for the absurdity of Christian beliefs about the end of the world, once again, even the pagan philosophers believed that the world would end in fire, and that there would be eternal life after death. And you may argue that fate controls our destinies, but even if that is true, it does not control our minds, and God judges us by our minds.

CHRISTIANS ARE HAPPIER IN MISFORTUNE THAN PAGANS IN PROSPERITY

How beautiful is the spectacle to God when a Christian does battle with pain; when he is drawn up against threats, and punishments, and tortures; when, mocking the noise of death, he treads under foot the horror of the executioner; when he raises up his liberty against kings and princes, and yields to God alone, whose he is; when, triumphant and victorious, he tramples upon the very man who has pronounced sentence against him! For the one who has obtained that for which he contends is the one who has conquered.

What soldier would not provoke peril with greater boldness under the eyes of his general? For no one receives a reward before his trial, and yet the general does not give what he does not have: he cannot preserve life, but he can make the warfare glorious. But God's soldier is neither forsaken in suffering nor brought to an end by death.

Thus the Christian may seem to be miserable; he cannot be really found to be so. You yourselves extol unfortunate men to the skies; Mucius Scaevola, for instance, who, when he had failed in his attempt against the king, would have perished among the enemies unless he had sacrificed his right hand.[9] And how many of our people have borne that not their right hand only, but their whole body, should be burned— burned up without any cries of pain, especially when they had it in their power to be sent away![10]

Do I compare men with Mucius or Aquilius, or with Regulus? Yet boys and young women among us treat with contempt crosses and tortures, wild beasts, and all the bugbears of punishments, with the inspired patience of suffering. . . .

We therefore, who are judged by our character and our modesty, reasonably abstain from evil pleasures, and from your pomps and exhibitions, the origin of which in connection with sacred things we know, and condemn their mischievous enticements.

For in the chariot games who does not shudder at the madness of the people getting into brawls?[11] Or at the teaching

---

[9] Captured by the enemy king, Scaevola stuck his hand in the fire to show how brave a Roman could be. The king was so impressed that he sent Scaevola back and made peace with Rome.

[10] Often, during the persecutions, a Christian could recant his faith at any point in the process and walk free.

[11] Like us, Romans had serious problems with sports hooliganism.

of murder in the gladiatorial games? In the scenic games also the madness is not less, but the debauchery is more prolonged: for now a mimic either expounds or shows forth adulteries; now nerveless player, while he feigns lust, suggests it; the same actor disgraces your gods by attributing to them adulteries, sighs, hatreds; the same provokes your tears with pretended sufferings, with vain gestures and expressions. Thus you demand murder in fact, while you weep at it in fiction.

CHRISTIANS ARE RIGHT TO BE HAPPY WITH SIMPLE JOYS

But that we despise the leavings of sacrifices, and the cups out of which libations have been poured, is not a confession of fear, but an assertion of our true liberty. For although nothing that comes into existence as an inviolable gift of God is corrupted by any agency, yet we abstain, in case anyone should think either that we are submitting to the demons to whom the libation has been made, or that we are ashamed of our religion.

But does anyone doubt that we indulge ourselves in spring flowers, when we gather both the rose of spring and the lily, and whatever else is of agreeable color and scent among the flowers? For these we both use scattered loose and free, and we twine our necks with them in garlands. Yes, please pardon us that we do not crown our heads; we are used to receiving the scent of a sweet flower in our nostrils, not inhaling it with the back of our head or with our hair.

Nor do we crown the dead. And in this respect you amaze me all the more, in the way in which you apply a torch to a lifeless person, or to one who does not feel—or a garland to one who does not smell it, when if he is blessed he does not want flowers, or if he is miserable he has no pleasure in them.

Still we adorn our funeral rites with the same tranquility with which we live; and we do not bind to us a withering garland, but we wear one living with eternal flowers from God, since we, being both moderate and secure in the liberality of our God, are roused to the hope of future happiness by the confidence of his present majesty. Thus we both rise again in blessedness, and are already living in contemplation of the future.

Then let Socrates the Athenian buffoon see to it, confessing that he knew nothing, although boastful in the testimony of a most deceitful demon; let Arcesilaus also, and Carneades, and Pyrrho, and all the multitude of the Academic philosophers, deliberate; let Simonides also for ever put off the decision of his opinion. We despise the bent brows of the philosophers, whom we know to be corrupters, and adulterers, and tyrants, and ever eloquent against their own vices.

We who bear wisdom not in our dress, but in our mind—we do not speak great things, but we live them; we boast that we have found what they were looking for with the utmost eagerness, and have not been able to find. Why are we ungrateful? Why do we grudge if the truth of divinity has ripened in the age of our time? Let us enjoy our benefits and let us in rectitude moderate our judgments; let superstition be restrained; let impiety be expiated; let true religion be preserved.

Caecilius is converted

When Octavius had ended his speech, for some time we were struck into silence, and held our faces fixed in attention. And as for me, I was lost in the greatness of my admiration, that he had so adorned those things which it is easier to feel than to say, both by arguments and by examples, and by authorities derived from reading; and that he had repelled the malevolent objectors with the very weapons of the philosophers with which they are armed, and had moreover shown the truth not only as easy, but also as agreeable.

While I was silently turning over these things in my own mind, Caecilius broke forth:

"I congratulate my Octavius as well as myself, as much as possible on that tranquility in which we live, and I do not wait for the decision. Even thus we have conquered: not unjustly do I assume to myself the victory. For even as he is my conqueror, so I am triumphant over error.

"Therefore, in what belongs to the substance of the question, I both confess concerning providence, and I yield to God; and I agree concerning the sincerity of the way of life which is now mine.

"Yet even still some things remain in my mind, not as resisting the truth, but as necessary to a perfect training of which on the morrow, as the sun is already sloping to his setting, we shall inquire at length in a more fitting and ready manner."

"As for me," I said, "I rejoice more fully on behalf of all of us; because Octavius has also conquered for me, in that I do not have to make either of you hate me by rendering a judgment. Nor can I acknowledge by my praises the merit of his words: the testimony both of man, and of one man only, is weak. He has an illustrious reward from God, inspired by whom he has pleaded, and aided by whom he has gained the victory."

After these things we departed, glad and cheerful: Caecilius, to rejoice that he had believed; Octavius, that he had succeeded; and I, that the one had believed, and the other had conquered.

—Minucius Felix, *Octavius (new translation)*

3.

BASIL OF CAESAREA AND GREGORY NAZIANZEN

IT WOULD BE WONDERFUL TO SAY that friendships are always delightful, that friends never feel betrayed, and that all you must do to be a good friend is to follow your conscience.

But it doesn't always work that way.

Sometimes friends have totally different ideas of what's right or what's important. They may have the best intentions, but one or the other—or both—can still damage the friendship just by being inflexible.

There's no better illustration than the fraught friendship of Basil of Caesarea and Gregory Nazianzen, two of the greatest thinkers in the history of the Church. They were college friends. In about 350, they were at Athens studying philosophy and rhetoric together, which was the equivalent of an Ivy League education.

By this time, the Roman Empire was safe for Christians. The emperors were Christians, at least nominally (they didn't always act like Christians, but that was another thing). But the basis of a good education was still the pagan philosophy and literature taught at Athens. It was a college town, and like every college town, it was full of temptations—as Gregory remembered:

> I'll leave it for someone else to tell how I came to Athens and education, and how I found the Christian teachers to be by far the wisest. All the young men seemed to be trying to outdo each other in wildness, but my course was like a stream of fresh water running through the brackish mud. I didn't get mired in the swamp: I was drawn to the better part. And that was where God gave me one more gift: he made me friends with the wisest man I've ever known.
>
> Yes, it was Basil, who has been the best thing that ever happened to me. Back then he was my closest friend. We lived together, we studied together, we learned together. I think I have a right to boast about how close we were. People knew us all over Greece. We had everything in common. We were one soul in two bodies. And what bound us together was the thought of God above and a longing for holy things. We trusted each other completely and poured out the deepest secrets of our hearts to each other.[1]

This sounds like the kind of friendship everyone hopes for. Gregory himself described it as an extraordinarily happy time. It was something almost like being in love—but much better, because it was a love of the spirit, based on spiritual things.

---

[1] This is a very free paraphrase of the poem translated in John Henry Newman, *The Church of the Fathers* (London: J. G. F. & J. Rivington, 1842), ch. 8.

And when, as time went on, we acknowledged our mutual affection, and that philosophy was our aim, we were everything to each other. We lived together, we ate together, we shared all our secrets. We had one object in life, and our affection for each other kept growing warmer and stronger.

Love for bodily attractions, since its objects are fleeting, is as fleeting as the flowers of spring. For the flame cannot survive, when the fuel is exhausted, and departs along with that which kindles it. Desire ends when its incentive wastes away.

But love that is godly and under restraint, since its object is stable, not only is more lasting, but, the fuller its vision of beauty grows, the more closely does it bind to itself and to one another the hearts of those whose love has one and the same object. This is the law of our superhuman love. . . .

We were impelled by equal hopes in the pursuit of letters, a pursuit that often provokes envy. Yet we knew no envy, and our rivalry was a healthy one. Each of us struggled, not to gain the first place for himself, but to yield it to the other; for we made each other's reputation to be our own. We seemed to have one soul living in two bodies. And if we must not believe those whose doctrine is "All things are in all," yet in our case it was believable, the way we lived in and with each other.

—Gregory of Nazianzus, Oration 43.20

But even though Basil and Gregory had a lot in common, they also had strong differences. Gregory was an introvert, and the kind of person who thought long and hard before he made a decision. Basil was the kind who made quick decisions and shoved his way through any opposition. Gregory seemed to have no personal ambition; as far as we can tell, his only goal was to live a good life as a good Christian. Basil wanted to change the world. Gregory could be bossed around by strong personalities. Basil was just the sort of strong personality who could boss people around.

St. John Henry Newman wrote a good description of the difference in character between these two saints—but also the striking similarities that brought them together as friends:

> This contrast of character, leading, first, to intimacy, then to differences, is interestingly displayed, though painfully, in one passage of the history of Basil and Gregory;—Gregory the affectionate, the tender-hearted, the man of quick feelings, the accomplished, the eloquent preacher,—and Basil, the man of firm resolve and hard deeds, the high-minded ruler of Christ's flock, the diligent laborer in the field of ecclesiastical politics. Thus they differed; yet not as if they had not much in common still; both had the blessing and the discomfort of a sensitive mind; both were devoted to an ascetic life; both were men of classical tastes; both were special champions of the Catholic creed; both were skilled in argument, and successful in their use of it; both were in highest place in the Church, the one Exarch of Caesarea, the other Patriarch of Constantinople.[2]

---

[2] Newman, *Church of the Fathers,* 117.

Having the same ideas about the Christian life, they both decided to withdraw from the world. They both came to the same conclusion: they didn't want to be surrounded by the world's evils and temptations, but they didn't want to be hermits, because that seemed selfish. So they would be monks.

Gregory explained his choice: "I saw that, when people live in this world of care, they do help other people, but in doing so they risk the calmness and pureness of their hearts. The ones who leave the world have a more righteous life and raise their eyes with quiet strength to heaven—but they only serve themselves, without brotherly love. And so I made my way between these two: I would meditate with the hermit, but live in the world and serve humanity."

As for Basil, he had lofty ideas of friendship, as he expressed them in letters to other correspondents:

> Just as mildew is a blight that grows in grain, so flattery stealing upon friendship is a blight of friendship.
>
> Even if my reason had not induced me to regard a man of such a character, our intimacy from boyhood would have sufficed to attach me to your soul. You know yourself how much custom has to do with friendship.
>
> I refuse to admit that I am in any way inferior to the men who have been famous for their friendship, for I have never been detected in any breach of mine. And, besides this, I have received from my God the commandment of love, and I owe you love not only as part of mankind in general, but because I recognize what you yourself have done both for my country and for me.
>
> —Basil, Letter 272

If I keep insisting on the privileges to which my superior age entitles me and wait for you to start talking to me, and if you, my friend, want to stick to your evil counsel of inaction more persistently—well, then, when will we ever talk to each other? However, where friendship is involved, I think being defeated is a victory. So I am quite ready to give you precedence and stop fighting about whose opinion is right.

—Basil, Letter 65 to Atarbius

And please don't be surprised at my calling my friend's property my own, for I have been taught the virtue of friendship along with the other virtues, and I remember the author of the wise saying, "A friend is another self." I therefore commend to your excellency this property that belongs to my friend as though it were my own.

—Basil, Letter 83 to a magistrate

You'd think it would have been easy for Gregory to maintain a friendship with a man who held to those principles. But in fact their relationship, strong as it was, ran into problems, and finally almost—but not quite—broke in pieces.

The first trouble came a few years after they left Athens, when Basil had become a monk, and Gregory still hadn't. "I have not kept my word, I admit it," he wrote to Basil. "Ever since Athens and our friendship and union of heart there, I have been saying that I would be your companion and follow a strict life with you. Yet I act against my wish, duty annulled by duty, the duty of friendship by the duty of filial reverence." His father needed him at home, he explained.

Basil was not pleased. In fact he spent the next few years trying to get Gregory into the monastic life with him.

But Gregory's father, the bishop of Nazianzus, had other plans. He needed his son's help administering the diocese, he said, so he insisted that Gregory be ordained a priest.

Gregory was not happy at all. But what could he do? A son owed obedience to his father, even if his father acted like a tyrant.

Meanwhile Basil ended up bishop of Caesarea. It was a hard time to be a Christian bishop. The Arian heresy, which insisted that the Son was a lesser being than the Father, had taken over much of the Church, partly because the emperors had been Arians for a while.

So Gregory and Basil were separated. Their friendship was kept up in letters—at least for a while. We do begin to see a little strain. Basil's letters seem a little impatient sometimes. Gregory, if anything, bends over backwards to keep a smile on his friend's face.

Soon politics began to take up much of Basil's time. Basil was bishop of Caesarea, the capital of Cappadocia. He was too powerful and popular for the Arian emperor, Valens, who took half of Cappadocia and made a new province out of it with its capital at Tyana. The bishop of Tyana, Anthimus, decided that this made him a metropolitan archbishop, equal in status to Basil, with authority over the bishops who had previously been under Basil.

With his friend in genuine difficulties, Gregory went to help Basil for a while. But he didn't stay long. Battles between bishops were not Gregory's thing.

And this is where we begin to see the strains really taking their toll on the friendship. Gregory had gone back to Nazianzus, and one of the monks there accused Basil of heresy. Gregory very publicly defended his friend, but at the same time he sent a letter to Basil asking him to explain his views more completely. And the idea that he had to explain anything to his best friend was very hurtful to Basil. It brings up Basil's long-simmering resentment: that Gregory had not stuck to their plan of going into a monastery together, and then had refused to stay with him in Caesarea to counterbalance the Arians. None of this would have happened, Basil says forthrightly, if you and I had been together.

I have received the letter of your religiousness, by the most reverend brother Hellenius; and what you have hinted, he has told me in plain terms. How I felt on hearing it, you cannot doubt at all. However, since I have decided that my affection for you will outweigh my pain, whatever it is, I have accepted it as I should, and I pray the Holy God that in my remaining days or hours I may be as fair to you as I have been in the past, during which, my conscience tells me, I have not neglected you in anything, small or great.

I understand that this man—who boasts that he is now just beginning to take a look at the life of Christians—thinks he will get some credit by having something to do with me. It is not at all surprising that he should invent what he has not heard and tell what he has never experienced. What *is* surprising and extraordinary is that he has got my best friends among the brethren at Nazianzus to listen to him; and not only to listen to him, but as it seems, to accept what he says.

On most grounds it might be surprising that the slanderer is of such a character, and that I am the victim, but these troubled times have taught us to bear everything with patience. Slights greater than this have, for my sins, long been things of common occurrence with me.

I have never yet given this man's brethren any evidence of my sentiments about God, and I have no answer to make now. Men who are not convinced by long experience are not likely to be convinced by a short letter. If the former is enough let the charges of the slanderers be counted as idle tales. But if I give license to unbridled mouths and uninstructed hearts to talk about anyone they like, all the while keeping my ears ready to listen, I shall not be alone in hearing what is said by other people; they will have to hear what I have to say.

I know what has led to all this and have urged every topic to hinder it; but now I am sick of the subject, and will say no more about it. I mean how little we see each other. For if we had kept our old promise to each other, and had due regard to the claims the churches have on us, we would have spent most of the year together—and then these slanderers would not have stood a chance.

Please, have nothing to say to them. Let me persuade you to come here and assist me in my labors, particularly in my contest with the individual who is now assailing me.[3] You can stop him just by showing up; as soon as you show these disturbers of our home that you will, by God's blessing, place yourself at the head of our party, you will break up their cabal, and you will shut every unjust mouth that speaks unrighteousness against God. And thus facts will show who are your followers in good, and who are the halters and cow-

---

[3]   He means Anthimus.

ardly betrayers of the word of truth.

If, however, the Church is betrayed—well, I will not try very hard to defend myself in words to people who judge me as people who have not yet learned to measure themselves would naturally judge. Perhaps, in a short time, by God's grace, I shall be able to refute their slanders by deed, for it seems likely that I shall have soon to suffer something more than usual for the truth's sake. The best I can expect is banishment—or, if this hope fails, after all, Christ's judgment-seat is not far distant.

So if you ask for a meeting for the churches' sake, I am ready to come wherever you invite me. But if it is only a question of refuting these slanders, I really have no time to reply to them.

—Basil, Letter 71

The conflict only got worse. What followed was an intricate chess game. Basil created more bishops in the area to counter the villain Anthimus. And Gregory offered his help because he recognized how big and important the battle was. But then he found out that Basil had taken advantage of his offer in a way Gregory never expected. Basil had made him bishop of Sasima, a one-horse town at a crossroads that had never had a bishop before.

The one thing Gregory never wanted to be was a bishop. He hadn't even wanted to be a priest, but being a bishop was a terrible responsibility—especially in unsettled times—and the last thing a man who wanted quiet above all could imagine getting involved in. And Basil hadn't even asked him first! He had just appointed Gregory a bishop to fill one of the squares on his chessboard.

Gregory had finally had enough. He went back home after only a short time in Sasima, and when Basil rebuked him, he burst out in a letter that carries the howl of a wounded friend down through the centuries. He thinks Basil cares only for principles and not at all for friends. And the worst thing of all is that he can't come up with any logical argument why Basil shouldn't act the way he's acting. If principles are really more important than friends, then—well, then go ahead. Be that way. That's really all Gregory can say.

Oh, stop talking about me as if I were an ignorant and uncouth man and a bad friend, not even worthy to live, because I've dared to be conscious of the way I've been treated. You yourself would admit that I haven't done anything else wrong, and my own conscience doesn't reproach me with having been unkind to you in anything, big or little. And I hope it never will.

I only know that I saw that I had been deceived—too late, true, but I saw it—and I throw the blame on your throne, because it lifted you above yourself. And I'm tired of being blamed for faults of yours, and of having to make excuses for them to people who know both our former and our present relations.

You know, of all I've had to endure this is the most ridiculous or pitiable thing, that the same person should have to suffer the wrong and also bear the blame. And this is what has happened to me. Different people blame me for different things, depending on their tastes, or their dispositions, or how much they resent me. But the kindest reproach me with contempt and disdain, and they throw me away after they've used me, like the most worthless containers, or those frames they build arches on, the ones that are taken down and thrown away when the building is finished.

Well, let them be and say what they like; no one can take away their freedom of speech. As my reward, pay off those blessed and empty hopes, which you devised against the evil speakers, who accused you of insulting me on pretense of honoring me, as though I were the kind of idiot who was easily taken in by such treatment.

Now I will tell you plainly what I'm thinking, and you must not be angry with me. I'll tell you just what I said at the moment of the suffering—and I wasn't so angry or astonished at what had happened that I lost my reason and didn't know what I was saying. I will not take up arms, nor will I learn tactics that I did not learn in former times, when the occasion seemed more suitable, as everyone was arming and in a frenzy (you know the illness of the weak), nor will I face the martial Anthimus, though he may be unprepared for the war, when I myself am unarmed and unwarlike, and thus more likely to get hurt. Fight with him yourself if you want to. Necessity often makes warriors even of the weak. Or look out for someone to fight when he seizes your mules, keeping guard over a mountain pass, and like Amalek of old, barring the way against Israel (see Exod 17).[4]

---

[4] This sounds like hyperbole, but Anthimus actually had done exactly that: he sent a gang of thugs to waylay Basil and his friends in a mountain pass when they were bringing back supplies from a farm that belonged to the diocese.

Give me quiet above all. Why should I fight for suckling pigs and poultry, and those not my own, as if I were fighting for souls and canons? Why should I deprive the Metropolis of the celebrated Sasima, or lay bare and unveil the secret of your mind, when I ought to join in concealing it?

So play the man. Be strong and make everything flow your way, the way the rivers pull in the winter floods, and don't worry about friendship or intimacy when you have high aims and piety to think about. Don't worry about the reputation you'll earn by acting this way. Give yourself up to the Spirit alone. I'll get one thing out of your friendship: I'll learn not to trust in friends, and not to think that there's anything more valuable than God.

—Gregory of Nazianzus, Letter 48

That was really the end of their friendship. There are a few more letters between them, but all of them are either irritable or strained. There's none of the natural affection, none of the witty banter, and none of the simple joy of knowing each other that we see in their earlier letters.

And Basil didn't have much longer to live. He died before he got to see the results of his manipulations.

But only days after he died, a new emperor came to the throne: Theodosius. He would be remembered as Theodosius the Great, the last great emperor for a long time. And Theodosius was an orthodox Catholic Christian.

And Gregory found himself bishop of Constantinople.

To be more accurate, at first he found himself *one* of the bishops of Constantinople. Constantinople very literally had more bishops than it knew what to do with. For forty years the Arians had dominated the city, and their bishop had been the most important one. But there was also a bishop of the Eunomians, a group that thought the other Arians were sellouts and really doubled down on the Jesus-is-not-God thing. And there was a bishop of the Novatians, a group that agreed with the orthodox Catholics about the divinity of the Son but had walked away when the Church decided to readmit Christians who lapsed under persecution. Each one of these claimed to be the only real Bishop of Constantinople. And now Gregory had to make his own claim.

As soon as Basil died, it seems as if Gregory turned into the powerhouse Basil had always wanted him to be. Since the Arians had all the churches in town, Gregory had to found his own church in his cousin's house. He called it the Church of the Resurrection—the place where the real Christian faith would be resurrected.

It was no fun being the Catholic bishop of a city where Arians had held sway for decades. Above all, Gregory wanted quiet, but instead he found himself in the middle of a constant riot. His preaching attracted huge crowds, and it also attracted mobs to beat him up. And of course, when he got beat up, the civil authorities charged him with inciting a riot.

But then Theodosius came to town, confirmed Gregory as bishop, and called an ecumenical council to sort out the mess. The Council of Constantinople reaffirmed what the Council of Nicaea had decided. Basil and Gregory had won. But some of the bishops tried to make trouble for Gregory, the president of the council, saying that his appointment as bishop of Constantinople had been irregular. Rather than stand and fight, the way Basil certainly would have done,

Gregory shocked everyone by resigning his bishopric in the middle of the council. The real victory was won anyway, and he could take a well-deserved rest.

It was three years after his friend Basil's death when Gregory finally made it back to Caesarea and delivered his famous memorial oration on his departed friend. He reminds his audience of Basil's almost superhuman accomplishments—not only in defending orthodox doctrine against heavy opposition but building practically a new city of charitable institutions to take care of the poor and sick. He tells the whole story of their friendship, too, much of which we've heard already.

Finally he comes to the thing that had killed their friendship. It still hurts, all these years later. And yet he can't help seeing it from his friend's point of view and understanding that Basil was doing what he thought was best. And from the point of view of the Church, Basil was probably right.

Let us see how great and wonderful his remedy was—or, I should say, how worthy of his soul. He made the dissension a cause of increase to the Church, and the disaster, under his very able management, resulted in the multiplication of the bishops of the country. From this, three very good things followed: a greater care for souls, the management by each city of its own affairs, and the end of the war in this quarter.

I am afraid that I myself was treated as an appendage to this scheme. I do not think I have to mince words with you. As much as I admire everything he did, more than I can say, I cannot praise this one particular thing. Yes, I will confess my feelings about it, since most of you know them already anyway.

I am talking about the change and faithlessness in the way he treated me. This is a wound that even time has not healed. For this is the source of all the inconsistency and tangle of my life; it has robbed me of the practice, or at least the reputation, of philosophy—though the reputation is hardly important.

But perhaps you will allow me to make this defense for him: his ideas were superhuman. Even before he died, he was already above worldly influences. His only interests were those of the Spirit. And his regard for friendship was not a bit lessened by his readiness to disregard its claims then, and *only* then, when they were in conflict with his paramount duty to God, and when the end he had in view was more important than the interests he was compelled to set aside.

That was how this great friendship ended: Gregory devastated by the loss of the friend he had never really reconciled with in life, and yet still clinging to some of the resentment he had felt for being a pawn in Basil's power game.

But it would be wrong to say that the friendship really ended there. Gregory was a Christian. He knew that the imperfect life here is only a prelude to the perfect life to come. And he had absolute confidence that Basil was still with him. There would come a time when they would be together, as they had always planned to be, though circumstances had temporarily stood in the way. At the end of his eulogy, Gregory spoke directly to his old friend.

This is my offering to you, Basil, spoken by the tongue that once was the sweetest of all to you, the tongue of the one who was your equal in age and rank. If I have come close to treating you the way you deserve, it is thanks to you, because I only started to speak out of confidence in you. But if it falls far short of your expectations, how do you suppose I must feel, when I am worn out with age and disease and regret for you? Still, God is pleased when we do what we can.

You can still gaze upon me from above, divine and sacred person that you are. Either use your prayers to take away that thorn in the flesh given to me by God for my discipline (see 2 Cor 12:7), or persuade me to bear it boldly, and guide all my life towards what is best for me. And if I do pass on, receive me there in your own tabernacle, so that, as we dwell together, and gaze together more clearly and more perfectly upon the holy and blessed Trinity, of which we have now in some degree received the image, our longing may at last be satisfied, by gaining this in return for all the battles we have fought and the assaults we have endured.

And that is what I have to say about you. But who will there be to praise me, since I leave this life after you—even if there is anything good to say about me?

In Christ Jesus our Lord, to whom be glory forever. Amen.

—Gregory of Nazianzus, Oration 43

4.

GREGORY OF NYSSA

THIS IS THE *OTHER* GREGORY. He was the brother of Basil of Caesarea, and if he was overshadowed by his more famous brother and his brother's friend Gregory, he wasn't overshadowed by *much*. He led a less spectacular life (although he, too, was sucked into his brother Basil's complicated chess game against Anthimus: that was probably why he was made bishop of Nyssa), but his theological writings were profound and have had a lasting influence on the Church.

Still, it wasn't all deep theology for Gregory. In this delightful little letter of introduction, he presents one friend to another who can be of benefit to the first. Who wouldn't want to help a man who came bearing such a charming letter from a close friend?

People of understanding admire [Alexander the Great], the king of the Macedonians, for one thing above all. For he is not admired so much for his famous victories over the Persians and Indians, and his penetrating as far the Ocean, as for his saying that he had his treasure in his friends.

In this respect I dare to compare myself with his marvelous exploits, and it will be right for me to say the same thing. I am rich in friendships. I may even be richer than that great man who was so proud of that very thing. Who was such a friend to him as you are to me, always trying to surpass yourself in every kind of excellence? No one would charge me with flattery. Just look at my age and your life. I'm too old for flattery, and it's not the time of life for me to worry about trying to please you. And as for you—well, even if it's always the right season to flatter you, praise wouldn't count as flattery. Your life praises you before my words get a chance.

But when we're rich in blessings, it's a special gift to know how to use what we have. When we have more than enough, the best thing to do is share it with our friends. Since my beloved son Alexander is, above all, a friend united to me in all sincerity, I hope you will show him my treasure—and not just show it to him, but put it at his disposal to enjoy abundantly. You can do that by giving him your help with what he has come to ask you about. He will explain it to you himself: that's better than me going into details in a letter.

—Gregory of Nyssa, Letter 5

5.

AMBROSE

Ambrose was a man who became a bishop against his will. He had been the much-respected Roman governor of the area that included Milan at a time when the Arian heresy was very powerful in the city, which was the imperial capital. When citizens gathered in the cathedral to choose a new bishop, it looked like a riot was breaking out between the orthodox and Arian factions. Ambrose ran in to try to keep the peace—and suddenly found himself surrounded by cries of "Ambrose for bishop!"

He tried to run away, but there was nowhere he could hide from an enthusiastic mob that wanted to make him bishop whether he liked it or not.

And he wasn't even a baptized Christian yet. He was still a catechumen, so he had to be baptized and ordained and raised to episcopal dignity almost all at once.

Well, if he was going to be a bishop, he was going to do it right. He gave away all his possessions and started studying. He already had a first-rate classical education, but he ended up one of the best Christian thinkers of his generation. Today we remember him not only for his own contributions, but also for being a friend and mentor to an even more famous thinker, St. Augustine.

When you must betray a friend

What if your friend is doing something wrong? So wrong that it could be a serious crime? How do you balance your duty to your friend with your duty to your country?

This is a hard question. Ambrose thinks friendship is a virtue, and one of the most important virtues there are. But we can't allow it to lead us *away* from virtue. So, yes, there could come a time when we must bear witness against a friend. But we must be very, very careful that we've done everything else we can do first.

Notice how Ambrose almost casually turns the old pagan ideas of friendship upside-down. He was certainly aware of what Cicero and such people had said about friendship—how there could be no friendship between people who weren't of equal status. But in a Christian world, the rules are different. God himself has called us friends, and that erases all the differences of class or wealth. It's true that those differences can be barriers in our imperfect world. But that's all the more reason to exercise the Christian virtue of humility, which can erase the difference between rich and poor.

We must never give up virtue for the sake of a friend. But if one must bear witness against a friend, it must be done with caution. Between friends what candor is needed in opening the heart, what magnanimity in suffering, what freedom in finding fault! Friendship is the guardian of virtues, which can only be found in people with similar characters. It must be mild in rebuking and averse to seeking its own advantage.

That is why true friends are rare among the rich. What is the dignity of friendship? The treachery of a friend is worse than the treachery of anyone else, and more hateful, too, as we see in the examples of Judas and Job's friends.

Still, nothing must be set before virtue. And to let us know that it may never be set aside by the desire for friendship, Scripture also gives us a warning on the subject of friendship. There are, indeed, various questions raised among philosophers: for instance, should you plot against your country for the sake of your friend, so as to serve your friend? Is it right to break your faith if it helps your friend?

And Scripture also says, "A man who bears false witness against his neighbor is like a war club, or a sword, or a sharp arrow" (Prov 25:18). But note what it adds. It does not blame witness given against a friend, but *false* witness. For what if the cause of God or of your country compels you to give witness? Should friendship take a higher place than our religion, or our love for our fellow citizens? In these matters, however, true witness is required so that a friend may not be assailed by the treachery of a friend, by whose good faith he ought to be acquitted. So we should never please a friend who desires evil, or plot against one who is innocent.

Certainly, if it is necessary to give witness, then, if you know of any fault in a friend, you should rebuke him secretly. If he does not listen, you must do it openly. For rebukes are good, and often better than a silent friendship. Even if a friend thinks himself hurt, still rebuke him; and if the bitterness of the correction wounds his mind, still rebuke him and fear not. "Faithful are the wounds of a friend; profuse are the kisses of an enemy" (Prov 27:6). So rebuke your straying friend; but do not forsake an innocent one. For friendship ought to be steadfast and to rest firm in true affection. We should not childishly change our friends at some idle whim.

Open your heart to a friend so that he may be faithful to you, and so that you may receive from him the delight of your life. "A faithful friend is an elixir of life; and those who fear the Lord will find him" (Sir 6:16). Give way to a friend as to an equal, and do not be ashamed to outdo your friend in doing kindly duties. For friendship knows nothing of pride. So the wise man says: "I will not be ashamed to protect a friend" (Sir 22:25). Do not desert a friend in time of need, or forsake him or fail him, for friendship is the support of life. Let us then bear our burdens as the Apostle has taught, for he spoke to those whom the charity of the same one body had embraced together (see Gal 6:2). If friends in prosperity help friends, why do they not also in times of adversity offer their support? Let us aid by giving counsel, let us offer our best endeavors, let us sympathize with them with all our heart.

If necessary, let us even endure hardship for a friend. Often we have to make enemies for the sake of a friend's innocence; we are often reviled if we defend and answer for a friend who is found fault with and accused. Do not be afraid of such displeasure, for the voice of the just says: "if some harm should happen to me because of him, whoever hears of it will beware of him" (Sir 22:26). In adversity, too, a friend is proved, for in prosperity all seem to be friends. But as in adversity patience and endurance are needed, so in prosperity strong influence is wanted to check and confute the arrogance of a friend who becomes overbearing.

How nobly Job when he was in adversity said, "Have pity on me, have pity on me, O you my friends" (Job 19:21). That is not like a cry of misery, but rather a cry of blame. For when he was unjustly reproached by his friends, he answered, "Have pity on me"—that is, you ought to show pity, but instead you assail and overwhelm a man with whose sufferings you ought to show sympathy for friendship's sake.

So, my children, preserve that friendship you have begun with your brethren, for nothing in the world is more beautiful than that. It is indeed a comfort in this life to have one to whom you can open your heart, with whom you can share confidences, and to whom you can entrust the secrets of your heart. It is a comfort to have someone you trust by your side, who will rejoice with you in prosperity, sympathize in troubles, encourage in persecution. What good friends those Hebrew children were whom the flames of the fiery furnace did not separate from their love of each other! (See Dan 3.) Of them we have already spoken. Holy David says well: "Saul and Jonathan, beloved and lovely! In life and in death they were not divided" (2 Sam 1:23).

This is the fruit of friendship; and so faith may not be put aside for the sake of friendship. You cannot be a friend to a human being if you have been unfaithful to God. Friendship is the guardian of pity and the teacher of equality, so as to make the superior equal to the inferior, and the inferior to the superior. For there can be no friendship between diverse characters, and so the goodwill of either ought to be mutually suited to the other. Let the inferior have authority if that is what is needed, and let the superior have humility. Let him listen to the other as though he were in the same position, an equal, and let the other warn and reprove like a friend, not from a desire to show off, but with a deep feeling of love.

Do not make your warning harsh or your rebuke bitter.

Friendship ought to avoid flattery, but it also ought to be free from arrogance. For what is a friend? Nothing but a partner in love, to whom you unite and attach your soul, and with whom you blend so as to desire to make one from two—to whom you entrust yourself as to a second self, from whom you fear nothing, and from whom you demand nothing dishonorable for the sake of your own advantage. Friendship is not meant as a source of revenue but is always appropriate and full of grace. Friendship is a virtue, not a way of making money. It is produced, not by money, but by esteem; not by the offer of rewards, but by a mutual rivalry in doing kindnesses.

Lastly, the friendships of the poor are generally better than those of the rich, and often the rich are without friends, while the poor have many. For true friendship cannot exist where there is lying flattery. Many try to please the rich by fawning all over them, but no one cares to make pretense to a poor man. Whatever is stated to a poor man is true, his friendship is free from envy.

What is more precious than friendship, which is shared alike by angels and by men? For that reason the Lord Jesus says, "make friends for yourselves by means of unrighteous mammon, so that when it fails they may receive you into the eternal habitations" (Luke 16:9). God himself makes us friends instead of servants, as he himself says: "You are my friends if you do what I command you" (John 15:14). He gave us a pattern of friendship to follow. We are to fulfill the wish of a friend, to unfold to him our secrets which we hold in our own hearts, and are not to disregard his confidences. Let us show him our heart and he will open his to us. Therefore Jesus says, "I have called you friends, for all that I have heard from my Father I have made known to you" (John 15:15). A friend, then, if he is a true one, hides nothing; he pours forth his soul as the Lord Jesus poured forth the mysteries of his Father.

So whoever does the will of God is his friend and is honored with this name. Whoever is of one mind with him is also his friend. For there is unity of mind in friends, and no one is more hateful than the man who injures friendship. Hence in the traitor the Lord found this the worst point on which to condemn his treachery, namely, that he gave no sign of gratitude and had mingled the poison of malice at the table of friendship. So he says: "But it is you, my equal, my companion, my familiar friend. We used to hold sweet converse together; within God's house we walked in fellowship" (Ps 55:13-14.) That is: it could not be endured, for you fell upon him Who granted grace to you. For if my enemy had reproached me, I could have borne it, and I would have hid myself from him who hated me. An enemy can be avoided; a friend cannot, if he desires to lay a plot. Let us guard against him to whom we do not entrust our plans; we cannot guard against him to whom we have already entrusted them. And so to show up all the hatefulness of the sin he did not say, "You, my servant, my apostle," but "you, a man of like mind with me"—that is, "You did not betray me, but yourself, for you betrayed a man of like mind with yourself."

The Lord himself, when he was displeased with the three princes who had not deferred to holy Job, wished to pardon them through their friend, so that the prayer of friendship might win remission of sins. Therefore Job asked and God pardoned. Friendship helped them whom arrogance had harmed (see Job 42:7-8).

These things I have left with you, my children, so that

you may keep them in mind. You yourselves will test whether they will be of any advantage.

—Ambrose, *On the Duties of the Clergy* 3.22.124–138

ACT LIKE A FRIEND AND PEOPLE WANT TO BE YOUR FRIEND

If people see us acting like true friends, says Ambrose, they want to be friends with us. If you need a practical reason to exercise the virtues of friendship with your own friends, here it is. Look at David, says Ambrose: people could see what a great friend he was, and so they supported him when Saul turned against him. Saul ruled by fear and failed; David ruled by love and succeeded.

Who would not have loved [David], when they saw how dear he was to his friends? For as he truly loved his friends, so he thought that he was loved as much in return by his own friends. Parents put him even before their own children, and children loved him more than their parents. That was why Saul was so angry and tried to hit his son Jonathan with a spear: because he thought that David's friendship held a higher place in his esteem than either filial piety or a father's authority.

It gives a very great impetus to mutual love if we show love in return to those who love us and prove that we do not love them less than we ourselves are loved—especially if we show it by the proofs that a faithful friendship gives. What is so likely to win favor as gratitude? What more natural than to love one who loves us? What is so implanted and so impressed on human feelings as the wish to let another, by whom we want to be loved, know that we love him? Well does the wise man say: "Lose your silver for the sake of a brother or a friend" (Sir 29:10). And again: "I will not be ashamed to protect a friend, and I will not hide from him" (Sir 22:25). If, indeed, the words in Sirach testify that the medicine of life and immortality is in a friend (see Sir 6:16), yet none has ever doubted that it is in love that our best defense lies. As the Apostle says: "Love bears all things, believes all things, hopes all things, endures all things. Love never ends" (1 Cor 13:7–8).

Thus David did not fail, for he was dear to all, and wished to be loved rather than feared by his subjects. Fear keeps watch for the time being but does not know how to keep guard permanently. And so where fear has departed, boldness often creeps in; for fear does not force confidence but affection calls it forth.

Love, then, is the first thing to give us a recommendation. It is a good thing therefore to have our witness in the love of many. Confidence comes from that, so that even strangers are not afraid to trust themselves to your kindness when they see you so dear to many. So likewise one goes through confidence to love, so that whoever has shown good faith to one or two has a kind of influence on the minds of all, and wins the good will of all.

—Ambrose, *On the Duties of the Clergy* 2.7.36–39

6.

AUGUSTINE

NO ONE had more complicated thoughts about friendship than Augustine, who died in the year 430 at the age of 75. That may be partly because we have so much of his writing, and over a long life his opinions must have developed. In fact, the scholar J. T. Lienhard identifies a definite progress in Augustine's thinking on the subject. In the beginning— fresh from his classical education—Augustine picked up Cicero's ideas almost verbatim, including Cicero's definition of friendship as "a perfect conformity of opinions upon all religious and civil subjects, united with the highest degree of mutual esteem and affection." But as Augustine matured, he began to see the complexities of the subject, and how they eluded Cicero. And he begins to see a new source of friendship. It's not the agreement on religious and civil subjects that makes friends. It's the grace God gives us that allows us to love others and become friends. That means the only *real* friendship is Christian friendship.[1]

Most people first meet Augustine in his *Confessions,*

---

[1] Joseph T. Lienhard, "Friendship in Paulinus of Nola and Augustine," *Augustiniana* 40, nos. 1–4 (1990): 291–94.

which has a good claim to be called the first real autobiography, in the modern sense of a history of the inner person more than the public deeds. This is where we hear the story of Augustine's childhood friend who was baptized on his deathbed. This was before Augustine converted, but the incident stuck in his mind. His analysis of his own grief is still both fascinating and heartbreaking after all these centuries

Notice that Augustine makes a distinction here in friendships. There is the friendship he had with this young man, which was delightful as far as it went. But there is also true friendship—which he could not have had then, because he wasn't yet a Christian.

In those years, when I first began to teach rhetoric in my native town, I had made a very dear friend. We had studied together. He was my age, and, like myself, just rising up into the flower of youth. He had grown up with me from childhood, and we had been both classmates and playmates.

No, he was not my *real* friend—not then, or even afterwards, as true friendship is; for there is no true friendship except in those that *you* bind together, holding onto you by that love which is "poured into our hearts through the Holy Spirit which has been given to us" (Rom 5:5).

But, still, it was very sweet, ripened as it was by the fervor of similar studies. He had been following the true faith but being young he had not soundly and thoroughly mastered it. I had turned him aside towards those superstitious and pernicious fables which my mother mourned in me. With me this man's mind now erred, nor could my soul exist without him.

But behold, *you* were close behind your fugitives—at once God of vengeance and Fountain of mercies, who turn us to you by wondrous means. You removed that man from this life when he had hardly completed one whole year of my friendship, sweet to me above all the sweetness of that life of mine.

Who can count all your praises, which he has experienced in himself alone? What was it that you did then, O my God, and how unsearchable are the depths of your judgments! For when, sore sick of a fever, he long lay unconscious in a death-sweat, and all despaired of his recovery, he was baptized without his knowledge. Meanwhile, I hardly cared, presuming that his soul would retain rather what it had imbibed from me, than what was done to his unconscious body. But it turned out completely differently, for he was revived and restored.

Immediately, as soon as I could talk to him (which I could as soon as he was able, for I never left him, and we hung too much upon each other), I tried to joke with him, as if he also would joke with me at that baptism which he had received when mind and senses were away from him, but had now learned that he had received. But he shuddered at me, as if I were his enemy; and, with a remarkable and unexpected freedom, admonished me, if I desired to continue his friend, to stop speaking to him in such a way. Confounded and confused, I concealed all my emotions, till he should get well, and his health be strong enough to allow me to deal with him as I wished.

But he was withdrawn from my frenzy, so that with you he might be preserved for my comfort. A few days after, during my absence, he had a return of the fever, and died.

At this sorrow my heart was completely darkened, and whatever I looked at was death. My native country was a torture to me, and my father's house a terrible unhappiness; and all the things I had done with him turned into frightful tortures without him. My eyes sought him everywhere, but he was not there. I hated all places because he was not in them; nor could they now say to me, "He'll be coming soon," as they did when he was alive and absent. I became a great puzzle to myself, and asked my soul why she was so sad, and why she disturbed me so much; but she had no answer for me. And if I said, "Hope in God," she very properly did not obey me; because that dearest friend she had lost was, as a man, both truer and better than that phantasm she was bid to hope in. Only tears were sweet to me, and they succeeded my friend in the dearest of my affections.

And now, O Lord, these things are passed away, and time has healed my wound. May I learn from you, who are Truth, and listen to you with the ear of my heart, so that you may tell me why weeping should be so sweet to the unhappy.

Though you are present everywhere, have you cast our misery far away from you? And you abide in yourself, but we are disturbed with various trials; and yet, unless we wept in your ears, there would be no hope for us remaining. How is it, then, that such sweet fruit is plucked from the bitterness of life, from groans, tears, sighs, and lamentations? Is it the hope that you hear us that sweetens it? This is true of prayer, for in prayer there is a desire to approach you. But is it also in grief for a thing lost, and the sorrow with which I was then overwhelmed? For I had no hope of his coming to life again, nor did I seek this with my tears; but I grieved and wept only, for I was miserable, and had lost my joy. Or is weeping a bitter thing, and for distaste of the things which we used to enjoy before, and even then, when we are loathing them, does it cause us pleasure?

But why do I speak of these things? For this is not the time to question, but rather to confess to you. I was miserable, as miserable as every soul fettered by the friendship of perishable things: he is torn to pieces when he loses them, and then is sensible of the misery he had before ever he lost them.

Thus was it at that time with me; I wept most bitterly, and found rest in bitterness. Thus was I miserable, and that life of misery I accounted dearer than my friend. For though I would willingly have changed it, yet I was even more unwilling to lose it than him. Indeed, I did not know whether I was willing to lose it even for him, as tradition tells us (if it is not an invention) of Pylades and Orestes, that they would gladly have died one for another, or both together, it being worse than death to them not to live together.

But there had sprung up in me some kind of feeling, too, contrary to this, for it was both exceedingly wearisome to me to live and dreadful to die. I suppose, the more I loved him, so much the more did I hate and fear, as a most cruel enemy, that death which had robbed me of him; and I imagined it would suddenly annihilate all men, as it had power over him.

That is how I remember feeling at the time. Behold my heart, O my God! Behold and look into me, for I remember it well, O my Hope! You clean me from the uncleanness of such affections, directing my eyes toward you, and pulling my feet out of the net.

For I was astonished that other mortals lived, since the one I loved, as if he would never die, was dead; and I wondered still more that I, who was to him a second self, could live when he was dead. Well did someone say of his friend, "You who are half of my soul," for I felt that my soul and his soul were but one soul in two bodies; and, consequently, my life was a horror to me, because I would not live in half. And that may be why I was afraid to die, because then the one I had loved so much would die completely.

O madness that knows not how to love men as men should be loved! O foolish man that I then was, enduring with so much impatience the lot of man!

So I fretted, sighed, wept, tormented myself, and took neither rest nor advice. I was carrying around with me a torn and polluted soul, impatient of being carried by me, and where to I found no place to rest it. Not in pleasant groves, not in sport or song, not in fragrant spots, not in magnificent banquets, not in the pleasures of the bed and the couch, nor, finally, in books and songs did it find repose. All things looked terrible, even the very light itself; and whatever was not my friend was repulsive and hateful—except groans and tears, for in those alone found I a little repose. But when my soul was withdrawn from them, a heavy burden of misery weighed me down.

It ought to have been raised to you, O Lord, for you to lighten it and take it away. I knew that but was neither willing nor able—all the more since, in my thoughts of you, you were not any solid or substantial thing to me. For you were not yourself, but an empty phantasm, and my error was my god. If I attempted to lay my burden on that god and let it rest, it sank into emptiness, and came rushing down again upon me, and I was left alone in an unhappy spot where I could neither stay nor leave. For where could my heart go to get away from my heart? Where could I fly from my own self? Where would I not follow myself? And yet I fled from my country; that way my eyes would look less for him where they were not accustomed to see him. And thus I left the town of Thagaste, and came to Carthage.

Time does not stand still, and it does not just pass through our senses without doing anything to us. It has strange effects on the mind. Time came and went from day to day, and by coming and going it put other ideas and other memories in my mind, and little by little patched me up again with the things I used to enjoy, and my sorrow gave way to them.

But there succeeded to it, not indeed other sorrows, yet the causes of other sorrows. For why had that recent sorrow so easily and deeply wounded me? It was because I had poured out my soul upon the dust, in loving one who must die as if he would never to die.

And what revived and refreshed me especially was the consolations of other friends, with whom I loved something else instead of *you*. And this was a monstrous fable and protracted lie [Manicheanism], which through the ears corrupted our itching minds by its adulterous scratching. And that fable would not die to me when any of my friends died.

There were other things in my friends that had more of an effect on my mind—to chat and laugh with them; to indulge in an interchange of kindnesses; to read pleasant books together; to joke together, and together to be grave; to disagree sometimes without ill-humor, as a man would do with his own self; and even by this disagreement in some few things to season, so to speak, and better relish our agreeing in many others; sometimes teaching, sometimes being taught; longing for the absent with impatience, and welcoming the coming with joy. These and similar expressions, emanating from the hearts of those who loved and were beloved in return, by the countenance, the tongue, the eyes, and a thousand pleasing movements, were so much fuel to melt our souls together, and out of many to make one.

This is what is loved in friends; and so loved that a man's conscience accuses itself if he does not love someone who loves him back, does not return the love of someone who loves him first, expecting nothing from him in the way of the flesh but indications of his love. Thus comes that mourning if a friend dies, and that gloom of sorrow, that steeping of the heart in tears, all sweetness turned into bitterness, and from the loss of the life of the dead even the death of the living. Blessed be he who loves you, Lord, and his friend in you, and his enemy for your sake. Only one who loves that way never loses anyone dear, since all are dear in him who cannot be lost. And who is this but our God, the God that created heaven and earth, and fills them, because by filling them he created them? No one loses except the one who leaves you. And whoever leaves you—where does he go, where can he run, but from you well pleased to you angry? For where does not he find your law in his own punishment? And your law is the truth, and that truth is yourself (John 14:6).

—Augustine, *Confessions* 4.4–9 (altered from the translations of Pusey and Challoner)

AUGUSTINE, JEROME, AND THE LETTER THAT CAME TOO LATE

St. Augustine is certainly one of the great minds in the history of the Church. St. Jerome is another. It's fascinating to realize that they lived at the same time and knew each other and considered each other friends.

But it was not an easy friendship to maintain. Jerome could be cranky and hard to get along with. His crankiness often comes out in his letters, and we can imagine that the letters were probably only a shadow of the man himself. Here's a fair sample:

> With his usual effrontery, Calphurnius, surnamed Lanarius, has sent me his execrable writings, which I understand that he has taken care to distribute in Africa also. To these I have made a short reply in the past; and I have sent you a copy of my treatise, intending by the first opportunity to send you a larger work, when I have leisure to prepare it. In this treatise I have been careful not to offend Christian feeling in any, but only to confute the lies and hallucinations arising from his ignorance and madness.[2]

I'm not going to be uncharitable about this, he says. I'm just going to tell him what an idiot he is.

As for Augustine, he could be difficult in his own way. He was very willing to admonish when he saw a need for admonishment. Jerome, for his part, was seldom very willing to be admonished. Put those two together, and you get an interesting and often entertaining correspondence.

The opposing stubbornnesses of Augustine and Jerome clashed most noisily in their long correspondence about a certain letter Augustine had written, in which he claimed that Jerome had made some theological errors. The letter was held up by circumstances, and Jerome found out about it in a

---

[2]   Letter 68 in Augustine's Letters.

way that was almost calculated to put him in a bad mood, as he explains in a letter to Augustine.

When my relative, our holy son Asterius, subdeacon, was just about to begin his journey, the letter of your Grace arrived, in which you clear yourself of the charge of having sent to Rome a book written against your humble servant. I had not heard that charge; but by our brother Sysinnius, deacon, copies of a letter that seems to be addressed to me by *someone* have come here.

In this letter I am urged to sing the *palinodia* [a poetic retraction], confessing my mistake in regard to a paragraph of the apostle's writing, and to imitate Stesichorus, who, vacillating between disparagement and praises of Helen, recovered, by praising her, the eyesight which he had forfeited by speaking against her.

Although the style and the method of argument appeared to be yours, I must frankly confess to your Excellency that I did not think it right to assume without looking into it that the letter was authentic, since I had seen only copies of it. Otherwise, if you were offended by my reply, you might justly complain that I should have made sure you were the author first, and answered you only after I was certain of that. . . .

Remember me, holy and venerable father. See how sincerely I love you, in that I am unwilling, even when challenged, to reply, and refuse to believe you to be the author of that which in another I would sharply rebuke. Our brother Communis sends his respectful salutation.

—Jerome to Augustine, Letter 68 in Augustine's letters

Already we can see Jerome's temper simmering under the surface. Augustine, who knew that temper well, could see it better than we can. And he knew that he *had* written that letter Jerome was so agitated about. He tried to tread delicately as the correspondence went on, explaining that the letter had been delayed by unforeseen circumstances in getting to Jerome. But Augustine was probably *too* delicate, and finally Jerome's temper boiled over.

You are sending me letter after letter, and often urging me to answer a certain letter of yours, a copy of which, without your signature, had reached me through our brother Sysinnius, deacon, as I have already written. You tell me that you entrusted this letter first to our brother Profuturus, and afterwards to someone else; but that Profuturus was prevented from finishing his intended journey, and having been ordained a bishop, was removed by sudden death; and the second messenger, whose name you do not give, was afraid of the perils of the sea, and gave up the voyage he had intended.

These things being so, I am at a loss to express my surprise that the same letter is reported to be in the possession of most of the Christians in Rome, and throughout Italy, and has come to everyone but me, to whom alone it was ostensibly sent. I wonder at this all the more, because that same brother Sysinnius tells me that he found it among the rest of your published works, not in Africa, not in your possession, but in an island of the Adriatic some five years ago.

True friendship can harbor no suspicion; a friend must speak to his friend as freely as to his second self. Some of my acquaintances, vessels of Christ, of whom there is a very large number in Jerusalem and in the holy places, suggested to me that you had not done this simply by mistake, but through desire for praise and celebrity, and notoriety in the eyes of the people. They said you intended to become famous at my expense, and did this so that many might know that you challenged me, and I feared to meet you; that you had written as a man of learning, and I had by silence confessed my ignorance, and had at last found one who knew how to stop my garrulous tongue.

But let me tell you frankly, the reason I refused to answer your Excellency at first was because I did not believe that the letter, or as I may call it (using a proverbial expression), the honeyed sword, was sent from you.

Moreover, I wanted to make sure I did not seem to answer discourteously a bishop of my own communion, and to censure anything in the letter of one who censured me, especially as I judged some of its statements to be tainted with heresy.

Lastly, I did not want to give you any reason to remonstrate with me, saying, "What! Had you seen the letter to be mine—had you discovered in the signature attached to it the autograph of a hand well known to you, when you so carelessly wounded the feelings of your friend, and reproached me with that which the malice of another had invented?"

So, as I have already written, either send me the exact letter in question signed with your own hand or stop annoying an old man who just wants retirement in his monastic cell. If you wish to exercise or display your learning, choose as your antagonists young, eloquent, and illustrious men, of whom I hear there are many in Rome who may be neither unable nor afraid to meet you, and to enter the lists with a bishop in debates concerning the Sacred Scriptures. As for me, a soldier once, but a retired veteran now, it becomes me rather to applaud the victories won by you and others, than with my worn-out body to take part in the conflict. If you persist in demanding a reply, well, look out—I might call to mind the history of the way in which Quintus Maximus by his patience defeated Hannibal, who was, in the pride of youth, confident of success.[3]

> Age bears all things away—the mind as well.
> When I was young I used to sing all day,
> But now I have forgotten all those songs.
> Even my voice has left me. [Virgil, *Eclogues* IX]

Or rather, to quote an instance from Scripture: Barzillai of Gilead, when he declined in favor of his youthful son the kindnesses of King David and all the charms of his court (see 2 Sam 19:34–37), taught us that old age ought neither to desire these things, nor to accept them when offered.

Now, you call God to witness that you had not written a book against me, and of course had not sent to Rome what you had never written—adding that, if by chance some things were found in your works in which a different opinion from mine was advanced, no wrong had thereby been done to me,

---

[3] When Hannibal invaded Italy with his Carthaginian army, Quintus Fabius Maximus wore him down by avoiding a pitched battle for years. Rome ultimately won the war, and Fabius earned the name *Cunctator,* "Delayer."

because you had, without any intention of offending me, written only what you believed to be right.

On that subject I beg you to hear me with patience.

You never wrote a book against me: how is it, then, that a copy has been brought to me, written by another hand, of a treatise containing a rebuke administered to me by you? How does Italy come to possess a treatise of yours that you did not write? Indeed, how can you reasonably ask me to reply to that which you solemnly assure me was never written by you?

Nor am I so foolish as to think that I am insulted by you, if in anything your opinion differs from mine. But if, challenging me as it were to single combat, you take exception to my views, and demand a reason for what I have written, and insist upon my correcting what you judge to be an error, and call upon me to recant it in a humble retraction, and speak of your curing me of blindness; in this I maintain that friendship is wounded, and the laws of brotherly union are nullified.

Don't let the world see us quarreling like children and giving material for angry contention between those who may become our respective supporters or adversaries. I write what I have now written, because I desire to cherish towards you pure and Christian love, and not to hide in my heart anything which does not agree with the utterance of my lips. For it does not become me, who have spent my life from youth until now sharing the arduous labors of pious brethren in an obscure monastery, to presume to write anything against a bishop of my own communion, especially against one whom I had begun to love before I knew him, who also sought my friendship before I sought his, and whom I rejoiced to see rising as a successor to myself in the careful study of the Scriptures.

So either disown that book, if you are not its author, and give up urging me to reply to that which you never wrote; or if the book is yours, admit it frankly; so that if I write anything in self-defense, the responsibility may lie on you who gave, not on me who am forced to accept, the challenge.

You say also, that if there is anything in your writings which has displeased me, and which I would wish to correct, you are ready to receive my criticism as a brother; and you not only assure me that you would rejoice in such proof of my goodwill toward you, but you earnestly ask me to do this. I tell you again, without reserve, what I feel: you are challenging an old man, disturbing the peace of one who asks only to be allowed to be silent, and you seem to desire to display your learning.

It is not for one of my years to give the impression of enviously disparaging one whom I ought rather to encourage by approbation. And if the ingenuity of perverse men finds something which they may plausibly censure in the writings even of evangelists and prophets, are you amazed if, in your books, especially in your exposition of passages in Scripture which are exceedingly difficult of interpretation, some things are found which are not perfectly correct?

This I say, however, not because I can at this time pronounce anything in your works to merit censure. First of all, I have never read them carefully; and in the second place, I do not have a supply of copies of what you have written here with me, excepting the books of *Soliloquies* and *Commentaries* on some of the Psalms; which, if I felt like criticizing them, I could prove to be at variance—well, I shall not say with my own opinion, for I am nobody, but with the interpretations of the older Greek commentators.

Farewell, my very dear friend, my son in years, my father in ecclesiastical dignity. I ask you to take care of one thing in particular. From now on, make sure *I'm* the first to receive any letters you write to me.

—Jerome to Augustine, Letter 72 in Augustine's letters

From this letter we learn that Jerome could be cranky, which is no news. But in his crankiness, he points out something valuable that might have escaped Augustine: friendship is not always *reasonable*. It may be perfectly *reasonable* for Augustine to point out where he thinks Jerome is wrong, but if he does it in a way that makes Jerome feel embarrassed, it damages their friendship—whether he's right or wrong about the intellectual question.

Augustine wrote back to Jerome to tell him that, yes, he had written that letter. But Augustine thinks that real friends ought to be able to separate the intellectual from the emotional. If Jerome disagrees with something Augustine wrote, then Augustine will be grateful to him for telling him he's wrong—even if he still believes he's right.

There can therefore be no doubt that you were prepared to reply in such a way as would offend me, if you had only indisputable evidence that the letter was mine. Accordingly, since I do not believe that you would think it right to offend me unless you had just cause, it remains for me to confess, as I now do, my fault as having been the first to offend by writing that letter which I cannot deny to be mine. Why should I strive to swim against the current, and not rather ask pardon? I therefore entreat you by the mercy of Christ to forgive me what I have done that has injured you, and not to render evil for evil by injuring me in return. For it will be an injury to me if you pass over in silence anything which you find wrong in either word or action of mine.

Of course, if you rebuke something in me that merits no rebuke, you do wrong to yourself, not to me; for far be it from one of your life and holy vows to rebuke merely from a desire to give offense, using the tongue of malice to condemn in me that which by the truth-revealing light of reason you know to deserve no blame. Therefore either kindly rebuke me when you think I merit rebuke, even if I am free from fault; or with a father's kindness soothe me when you cannot bring me to agree with you. For it is possible that your opinion may be at variance with the truth, while notwithstanding your actions are in harmony with Christian charity: for I also shall very thankfully receive your rebuke as a most friendly act, even if the thing you censured could be defended and therefore ought not to have been censured; or else I shall acknowledge both your kindness and my fault, and shall be found, so far as the Lord enables me, grateful for the kindness, and corrected in the fault.

—Augustine to Jerome, Letter 73 in Augustine's letters

Augustine and Paulinus: The pattern of Christian friendship

Paulinus of Nola was a rich senator who gave up everything to live an ascetic life. Augustine and Paulinus became great friends through letters, even though they had never met. Paulinus thought a real Christian could be happy to have such a spiritual friendship, but Augustine insisted that seeing a friend in person was still a big part of friendship.

O excellent man and excellent brother, there was a time when you were unknown to my mind; and I tell my mind to bear patiently your being still unknown to my eyes, but it almost—well, I should say completely—refuses to obey.

Does it indeed bear this patiently? If so, why then does a longing for your presence rack my inmost soul? For if I were suffering bodily infirmities, and these did not interrupt the serenity of my mind, I might be justly said to bear them patiently; but when I cannot bear with equanimity the privation of not seeing you, it would be intolerable if I were to call my state of mind patience.

Nevertheless, it would perhaps be still more intolerable if I were to be found patient while absent from you, seeing that you are the sort of person you are. It is a good thing, therefore, that I am unsatisfied—because if I were satisfied with this privation, everyone would justly be dissatisfied with me.

What has happened to me is strange, yet true: I grieve because I do not see you, and my grief itself comforts me; for I neither admire nor covet a fortitude easily consoled under the absence of good men such as you are. For do we not long for the heavenly Jerusalem? And the more impatiently we long for it, do we not the more patiently submit to all things for its sake? Who can so withhold himself from joy in seeing you, as to feel no pain when you are no longer seen? I at least can do neither; and seeing that if I could, it could only be by trampling on right and natural feeling, I rejoice that I cannot, and in this rejoicing, I find some consolation. It is therefore not the removal, but the contemplation, of this sorrow that consoles me.

Do not blame me, I beg you, with that devout seriousness of spirit that so eminently distinguishes you. Do not say that I do wrong to grieve because of my not yet knowing you, when you have disclosed to my sight your mind, which is the inner man. For if, when traveling in any place, or in the city to which you belong, I had come to know you as my brother and friend, and as one so eminent as a Christian, so noble as a man, how could you think that it would be no disappointment to me if I were not permitted to know your dwelling? How, then, can I do anything but mourn because I have not yet seen your face and form, the dwelling-place of that mind which I have come to know as if it were my own?

In this same letter, Augustine gives us a glimpse of what he thinks a good Christian friend is like—a glimpse that helps explain some of his difficulties with Jerome. Augustine thinks Christian friends should not be afraid to reprove each other. If you see something wrong with me, he says, you should tell me. In this case, Augustine is expecting that Paulinus is about to read all the books Augustine has written so far, and he wants to make it clear that Paulinus should be forthright in pointing out any errors. As we saw, this is exactly what he would tell Jerome—but we already know how that went over.

This is a very important point to Augustine, however. The clergy administer the Sacrament of Reconciliation. But for Augustine, all Christians share in that mission, as the scholar Joseph Carola points out. *Fraternal correction* is our business, and we all in some degree share that wonderful gift and awful responsibility Christ gave the Apostles: "If you forgive the sins of any, they are forgiven; if you retain the sins of any, they are retained" (John 20:23).[4]

But when you are reading these, my holy Paulinus, let not those things which Truth has spoken by my weak instrumentality carry you away so much that they prevent you from carefully observing what I myself have spoken. If you drink in with eagerness the things good and true which have been given to me as a servant, I do not want you to forget to pray for the pardon of my errors and mistakes. In anything you see that justly displeases you, you are seeing me myself; but in anything in my books that you approve, through the gift of the Holy Spirit bestowed on you, you should love and praise the One with whom is the fountain of life, and in whose light we shall see light, not darkly as we do here, but face to face

---

[4] Joseph Carola, *Augustine of Hippo: The Role of the Laity in Ecclesial Reconciliation* (Rome: Editrice Pontificia Università Gregoriana, 2005), 153–54.

(see 1 Cor 13:12). When I read over my writings and discover anything that is due to the working of the old leaven in me (see 1 Cor 5:7), I blame myself for it with true sorrow; but if anything that I have spoken is, by God's gift, from the unleavened bread of sincerity and truth, I rejoice with trembling.

—Augustine to Paulinus, Letter 27 in Augustine's letters

The joy and pain of friendship

Near the end of his life, as the world seemed to be overwhelmed with calamities, and old age took away the friends that violence had spared, Augustine meditated on the strange combination of joy and bitterness that comes with friendship. We can hardly go on living without friends—and yet how much pain it gives us just to worry about them! The only consolation when we do lose them is to remember that they are now spared the pain and uncertainty we are still suffering.

In our present wretched condition, we frequently mistake a friend for an enemy, and an enemy for a friend. And if we escape this pitiable blindness, is not the unfeigned confidence and mutual love of true and good friends our one solace in human society, filled as it is with misunderstandings and calamities?

And yet the more friends we have, and the more widely they are scattered, the more numerous are our fears that some portion of the vast masses of the disasters of life may light upon them. For we are not only worried that they might suffer from famine, war, disease, captivity, or the inconceivable horrors of slavery, but we are also affected with the much more painful dread that their friendship may be changed into perfidy, malice, and injustice.

And when these possibilities actually do happen—and they happen more frequently the more friends we have, and the more widely they are scattered—and when we find out about them, who but one who has experienced it can tell with what pangs the heart is torn? We would really prefer to hear that they were dead, although we could not hear of that without anguish. For if their life has consoled us with the charms of friendship, can it be that their death should affect us with no sadness?

Whoever wants to have none of this sadness must, if possible, have no friends at all. Let him prohibit or extinguish friendly affection; let him burst with ruthless insensibility the bonds of every human relationship; or let him contrive so to use them that no sweetness shall distill into his spirit.

But if this is utterly impossible, how shall we contrive to feel no bitterness in the death of those whose life has been sweet to us? And so comes that grief which affects the tender heart like a wound or a bruise, and which is healed by the application of kindly consolation. For though the cure is made all the more easily and rapidly the better condition the soul is in, we must not on this account suppose that there is nothing at all to heal.

So, although our present life is afflicted (sometimes more mildly, sometimes less) by the death of those very dear to us, and especially of useful public men, yet we would prefer to hear that such men were dead rather than to hear or perceive that they had fallen from the faith, or from virtue—in other words, that they were spiritually dead. Of this vast material for misery the earth is full, and therefore it is written, "Has not man a hard service upon earth?" (Job 7:1). And with the same reference the Lord says, "Woe to the world for temptations to sin!" (Matt 18:7). And again, "And because wickedness is multiplied, most men's love will grow cold" (Matt 24:12).

So we enjoy some satisfaction when our good friends die; for though their death leaves us in sorrow, we have the consoling assurance that they are beyond the ills by which in this life even the best are broken down or corrupted, or are in danger of both.

—Augustine, *The City of God* 19.8

7.

JOHN CHRYSOSTOM

St. John Chrysostom was about the same age as St. Augustine, and he wrote almost as much as Augustine did. He came from Antioch, the big city at the eastern end of the Mediterranean. There he got a first-rate education from both pagan and Christian teachers, so he knew both the Scriptures and classical Greek literature backwards and forwards.

John's ambition was to be a hermit, and he lived that way for a few years. But his talents were too bright to hide under a bushel. In spite of himself, he became the most famous preacher in the East, earning the nickname "Chrysostom"— the Man with the Golden Mouth. His sermons were the chief popular entertainment in Antioch.

So when the imperial government wanted a celebrity preacher to be archbishop of Constantinople, the choice was obvious. Unfortunately for everyone, Chrysostom didn't play well with rich people. He was perfectly willing to scold the Empress for showing up in fine clothes when people were starving in the streets. The common people loved him, but eventually he made so many of the powerful hate him that he was thrown out of the city. He died in 407 on his way from exile to even more remote exile, because if even a letter from

John Chrysostom reached Constantinople, it caused a dangerous popular commotion.

Do your friends see a Christian when they look at you?

How do you explain the Christian life to your non-Christian friends? In a funny passage, St. John Chrysostom imagines a dialogue between a pagan and a Christian that answers this question. Yes, you can go ahead and tell your "Gentile" friend (as Chrysostom calls the unbelievers) what Christianity is, but it will do no good unless you live the Christian life in a way that everyone can see.

And do not think only about what you will *say* to the Gentile. Think, too, about how you will live a better life yourself. When he is offended by looking at the way you live, then consider what you will say. For if he is offended, you will not be called to a reckoning for him, but if it is your way of life by which he is injured, you will have to undergo the greatest danger.

When he sees you philosophizing about the kingdom and fussing about the things of this life—when he sees you afraid about hell and trembling at the calamities of this life at the same time—then think about it! He will accuse you and say, "If you are in love with the Kingdom, how is it you do not look down on the things of this life? If you are expecting the awful judgment, why do you not despise the terrors of this world? If you hope for immortality, why do you not scorn death?"

When he says this, you had better worry about what defense you will make. When he sees you trembling at the thought of losing your money—you who expect the heavens!—and exceedingly glad about a single penny, and selling your soul again for a little money, then think about it! For these are the things, precisely these, that make the Gentiles stumble.

And so, if you care about his salvation, make your defense on these subjects, not by words, but by actions. No one ever blasphemed God through that question. No, it is because of the way we live that there are thousands of blasphemies everywhere.

Set him right then. For the Gentile will next ask you, "How can I know that God's commands are even possible? You came from a Christian family and have been brought up in this fine religion—but you don't follow them at all!"

And what will you tell him?

You will be sure to say, "I will show you others that do: monks who live in the deserts."

And are you not ashamed to confess to being a Christian, and yet to send him to others because you cannot convince him that you live like a Christian?

For he also will say directly, "Why should I go to the mountains and track down people in the deserts? If there is no way a person who is living in the midst of cities can be a disciple, this is a sad reflection on this rule of conduct, that we are to leave the cities, and run to the deserts. But show me a man who has a wife, and children, and family, and still pursues wisdom."

What are we then to say to all this? Must we not hang down our heads, and be ashamed? For Christ gave us no such commandment. But what *did* he say? "Let your light shine before *men*" (Matt 5:16)—not mountains, and deserts, and wildernesses, and out-of-the-way places. And I say this not to abuse those who have taken up with the mountains, but to bewail those who live in cities, because they have banished virtue from the city!

So I beg you, let us take the discipline they have there and bring it here also, so that the cities may become cities indeed. This will improve the Gentile. This will free him from countless offenses.

—John Chrysostom, Homily 26 on Romans 14:23

MAKING FRIENDS SHOULD BE YOUR VOCATION

Nothing is more powerful than Christian friendship, Chrysostom says. If only a few of us really made it our *job* to make friends, there would be no stopping us.

And how do we do that?

We love. We love others whether they love us or not. We don't keep accounts of how much they loved us back. If they never become our friends, so much the worse for them. But just for trying we earn a great reward.

For us, there is nothing good without friendship. Let there be good things without number, but what is the benefit—be it wealth, be it luxury—without friendship? No possession is equal to this, even in matters of this life, just as there is nothing worse than being hated. . . .

We have one world that we all live in, we are all fed with the same fruits. But these are small things! By the same Sacraments we partake of the same spiritual food. These surely are justifications of loving! Think how many reasons for friendship people outside the Church have thought up: having the same art or trade, neighborhood, or relationships—but mightier than all these are the impulses and ties we have. This Table is better designed to shame us into friendliness.

But many of us who come to it do not even know one another. The reason, it may be said, is that there are so many of us. That's not true; it is only our own sluggish indifference. There were three thousand (Acts 2:41)—there were five thousand (Acts 4:4)—and yet they had all one soul. But now each knows not his brother and is not ashamed to lay the blame on the number, because it is so great!

Yet whoever has many friends is invincible against all men: he is stronger than any tyrant. The tyrant does not have as much safety with his bodyguards as this man has with his friends. And besides, this man is more glorious than the tyrant: for the tyrant is guarded by his own slaves, but this man by his equals: the tyrant, by men unwilling and afraid of him; this man by willing men and without fear.

And here too is a wonderful thing to be seen—many in one, and one in many. Just as in a harp, the sounds are diverse, not the harmony, and they all together give out one harmonious chord, I could wish to bring you into such a city, if it were possible, in which all would be one soul. Then you would see a more harmonious music, better than any harmony from harp or flute! But the musician is the power of Love: it is this that strikes out the sweet melody, singing, a strain in which no note is out of tune. This strain rejoices both Angels, and God the Lord of Angels; this strain rouses the whole audience that is in heaven; this even lulls the passions—it does not even allow them to be raised, but deep is the stillness. For as in a theater, when the band of musicians plays, all listen with a hush, and there is no noise there; so among friends, while Love strikes the chords, all the passions are still and laid to sleep, like wild beasts charmed and pacified: just as, where hate is, everything is the reverse. But let us say nothing just now about enmity; let us speak of friendship.

Even if you say something hasty, there is no one to catch you up, but all forgive you; even if you do something hasty, no one thinks the worst of it, but all allowance is made: everyone is prompt to stretch out the hand to anyone who is falling, everyone wants him to stand. It is an unbreachable wall, this friendship; a wall that even the devil himself cannot break down, much less human beings. It is not possible for a man to fall into danger if he has many friends.

There is no room for anger, but only for good feelings: no room for envy, none for resentment. Look at the man with many friends. See how he does everything easily, both spiritual and temporal. What then, I ask you, can be equal to this man? Like a city walled on every side is this man, the other as a city unwalled.

Great wisdom, to be able to be a creator of friendship! Take away friendship, and you have taken away all, you have confounded all.

But if even the *appearance* of friendship has such great power, what must the reality itself be? Then let us, I beseech you, make friends for ourselves, and let each make this his art.

But, look, you will say, I *am* trying to be friends, but the others aren't! Well, all the greater the reward to you.

True, say you, but it's harder than you think.

How? I ask. Let me tell you right now, if only ten of you would knit yourselves together, and make this your work—in the same way the Apostles made preaching their work, and the Prophets teaching, if we made making friends our job— great would be the reward. Let us make royal portraits for ourselves. For if this is the common badge of disciples, then we are doing a greater work than if we should put ourselves into the power to raise the dead. The diadem and the purple mark the Emperor, and where these are not, though his apparel be all gold, the Emperor is not yet manifest. So now you are making known your lineage. Make men friends to yourself and to others. No one who is loved will wish to hate you. Let us learn the colors, with what ingredients they are mixed to make up this portrait. Let us be affable: let us not wait for our neighbors to move. Don't say, "If I see anyone holding off, I'll hold off more than he does." No, go right up to him and extinguish his bad feeling. If you saw someone who was sick, would you make him sicker?

This, most of all, let us make sure of—to "outdo one another in showing honor" (Rom 12:10), to "count others better than yourselves" (Phil 2:3). Don't think you're putting yourself down. If you give someone else honor, you have honored yourself more. You have made yourself even more distinguished. On all occasions let us yield the precedence to others. Let us bear nothing in mind of the evil done to us, but only think of any good done to us. Nothing so makes a man a friend, as a gracious tongue, a mouth speaking good things, a soul free from self-elation, a contempt of vainglory, a despising of honor. If we secure these things, we shall be able to become invincible to the snares of the devil, and having with strictness accomplished the pursuit of virtue, to attain unto the good things promised to them that love him, through the grace and mercy of our Lord Jesus Christ, with Whom to the Father and the Holy Ghost together be glory, dominion, honor, now and ever, world without end. Amen.

—John Chrysostom, Homily 40 on the Acts of the Apostles

YOU ARE MY FRIENDS

What does it mean when Jesus tells his disciples that they are his friends? It means real friendship. Like a friend, he tells them everything. Like a friend, he does everything he can do for them, even dying for them. And like a friend, he shares everything he has with them and is always there when they need him.

"You are my friends if you do what I command you. No longer do I call you servants, for the servant does not know what his master is doing; but I have called you friends, for all that I have heard from my Father I have made known to you" (John 15:14–15).

Then why does he say, "I have yet many things to say to you, but you cannot bear them now" (John 16:12)? When he says "all" and "heard," all he means is that he said nothing foreign, but only what was of the Father. And since to speak of secrets appears to be the strongest proof of friendship, you have, he says, been deemed worthy even of this communion. When, however, he says "all," he means, "Whatever things it was fit that they should hear."

Then he gives another sure proof of friendship, an extraordinary one. What do I mean?

"You did not choose me, but I chose you" (John 15:16).

That is, I ran to your friendship. And he didn't stop there, but, "I appointed you," he says (that is, I planted you), "that you should go and bear fruit" (he still uses the metaphor of the vine)—that is, that you should extend yourselves—"and that your fruit should abide" (John 15:16).

Now if your *fruit* abides, much more shall *you* abide. For I have not only loved you, he says, but have done you the greatest benefits, by extending your branches through all the world.

Do you see in how many ways he shows his love? By telling them things secret, by having in the first instance run to meet their friendship, by granting them the greatest blessings, by suffering for them what then he suffered. After this, he shows that he also remains continually with those who shall bring forth fruit; for it is needful to enjoy his aid, and so to bear fruit.

—John Chrysostom, Homily 77 on John

Keep your friends out of trouble

Are your friends getting themselves into things they shouldn't? That's when they need you. Argue with them. Make them feel ashamed. Grab them by the shirt if you must.

Whatever it takes, keep them out of trouble. And let them know you expect the same treatment from them.

"But I'm no speaker," you say. But you don't need to be eloquent. If you see a friend going into fornication, say to him, "You are going after a bad thing! Aren't you ashamed? Don't you blush? This is wrong!"

"Why?" you say. "Doesn't he know it's wrong?" Yes, but he is dragged on by lust. Those who are sick also know that it is bad to drink cold water; nevertheless, they need people to keep them from it.[1] For one who is suffering will not easily be able to help himself in his sickness. He needs someone healthy—you—for his cure. And if he isn't persuaded by your words, watch for him as he goes away and hold onto him; perhaps he will be ashamed.

"And what good does it do," you say, "when he does this just for my sake, because he has been held back by me?" Don't overthink this. For a while, by whatever means, keep him away from his evil practice; let him get used to not going off to that pit, whether through you or through any other means. When you have gotten him used to not going, then by taking him after he has caught his breath a little you will be able to teach him that he ought to do this for God's sake, and not for man's. Don't try to fix everything at once, since you can't: but do it gently and by degrees.

---

[1] We wouldn't take Chrysostom's outdated medical advice today, but the point stands: our friends need help to do what they know is good for them.

If you see him going off to drinking, or to parties where there is nothing but drunkenness, then also do the same; and again on the other hand beg him, if he observes that you have any failing, to help you and set you right. For in this way, he will even bear reproof of his own free will, when he sees both that you need reproofs as well, and that you help him, not as one that had done everything right, nor as a teacher, but as a friend and a brother. Say to him, "I have helped you out, in reminding you of what was right: now you, too, whatever failing you see in me, hold me back, set me right. If you see me irritable or avaricious, restrain me, bind me by persuasion."

This is friendship; thus "A brother helped is like a strong city" (Prov 18:19). It isn't eating and drinking that make friendship: even robbers and murderers have friendship like that. But if we are friends, if we truly care for one another, let us in these respects help one another. This leads us to a profitable friendship: let us hinder those things which lead away to hell.

—John Chrysostom, Homily 30 on Hebrews

FRIENDSHIP IS THE BEST MEDICINE AGAINST HERESY

What causes schism and heresy? Chrysostom finds the root of it in a simple lack of Christian love. If you exercise the virtues of friendship, you won't be so stuck on yourself that you'd rather separate from all your sisters and brothers in the Church than admit you might be wrong.

"The aim of our charge is love that issues from a pure heart and a good conscience and sincere faith. Certain persons by swerving from these have wandered away into vain discussion, desiring to be teachers of the law, without understanding either what they are saying or the things about which they make assertions" (1 Tim 1:5-7).

Nothing is worse for humanity than to undervalue friendship, and not to cultivate it with the greatest care—just as nothing, on the other hand, is so beneficial, as to pursue it to the utmost of our power. Christ shows us this when he says, "if two of you agree on earth about anything they ask, it will be done for them by my Father in heaven" (Matt 18:19); and again, "because wickedness is multiplied, most men's love will grow cold" (Matt 24:12).

This is what has caused every heresy. For men, because they did not love their brethren, have envied those who were in high repute, and from envying, they have become eager for power, and from a love of power have introduced heresies. This is why, after Paul has said, "that you may charge certain persons not to teach any different doctrine" (1 Tim 1:3), now he shows that the way to do this is through love. So when he says, "Christ is the end of the Law" (Rom 10:4)—that is, its fulfillment, and this is connected with the former, in the same way this commandment is implied in love. The end of medicine is health, but where there is health, there is no need to worry much about medicine. So where there is love, there is no need of much commanding.

But what sort of love does he speak of? That which is sincere, which is not merely in words but which flows from the disposition, from sentiment, and sympathy. "From a pure heart," he says, either with respect to a right conversation, or sincere affection. For an impure life too produces divisions. "For every one who does evil hates the light" (John 3:20). There is indeed a friendship even among the wicked. Robbers and murderers may love one another, but this is not from a good conscience, not from a pure but from an impure heart, not from sincere faith but from that which is false and hypocritical. For faith points out the truth, and a sincere faith produces love, which he who truly believes in God cannot endure to lay aside.

—John Chrysostom, Homily 2 on 1 Timothy

When should you lie to your friends?

Chrysostom's dialogue *On the Priesthood* disturbs many readers, and for good reason. It seems to be making an argument that any deception is not only acceptable but virtuous if it leads our friends on the right path.

Can that really be true? Can it really be Christian?

The story, as Chrysostom sets it up, is this: he had a friend named Basil, and the people wanted to make them both bishops. (More than once we read about one of the Fathers who was made a bishop against his will, practically by mob violence—remember the case of Ambrose.) Chrysostom allowed his friend to believe he had accepted his own episcopal seat—and then got away clean while his friend had to be a bishop.

Naturally, his friend was put out about that.

Chrysostom argues that he used the deception for good: his friend will be a good bishop, whereas he himself would be a lousy one.

But the fact that Chrysostom—who usually argues his points very persuasively—leaves us wondering whether he's right may mean that he's aiming at something more than just a simple message here. The dialogue format gives his friend Basil ample opportunity to voice his objections, and Basil walks away feeling worse than before—not the usual result in a Christian writer's dialogue. The safest thing we can say is that the question is very difficult, and Chrysostom—who portrays himself as a naive young man in the dialogue—seems, as the writer, to be completely aware of the difficulties.

I had many genuine and true friends, men who understood the rules of friendship, and faithfully observed them; but out of this large number there was one who excelled all the rest in his attachment to me, striving to outstrip them as much as they themselves outstripped ordinary acquaintance. He was one of those who were constantly at my side; for we were engaged in the same studies and employed the same teachers. We had the same eagerness and zeal about the studies at which we worked, and a passionate desire produced by the same circumstances was equally strong in both of us. Not only when we were at school, but even after we had left it, when we had to decide what course of life it would be best for us to adopt, we found ourselves to be of the same mind.

And in addition to these, there were other things also which preserved and maintained this agreement unbroken and secure. Neither one of us had a reason to brag that our country was better than the other's. I was not weighed down with riches, and he was not pinched by poverty, but our means corresponded as closely as our tastes. Our families also were of equal rank, and thus everything went along with our disposition.

But when it became our duty to pursue the blessed life of monks, and the true philosophy, our balance was no longer even, but his scale mounted high, while I, still entangled in the lusts of this world, dragged mine down and kept it low, weighting it with those fancies in which youths are apt to indulge. For the future, our friendship indeed remained as firm as it was before, but our intercourse was interrupted; for it was impossible for two people who were not interested in the same things to spend much time together.

But as soon as I also began to emerge a little from the flood of worldliness, he received me with open arms. Even so, we were not able to keep up our former equality: for since he had a head start, and had pursued his goal very enthusiastically, he rose again above my level, and soared to a great height.

Being a good man, however, and placing a high value on my friendship, he separated himself from all the rest, and spent all his time with me—which he had wanted to do before, but had been prevented (as I was saying) by my frivolity. For it was impossible for a man who attended the law-courts, and was in a flutter of excitement about the pleasures of the stage, to be often in the company of one who was nailed to his books, and never set foot in the marketplace. So when the hindrances were removed, and he had brought me into the same condition of life as himself, he gave free vent to the desire with which he had long been laboring. He could not bear leaving me even for a moment, and he persistently urged that we should each of us abandon our own home and share a common dwelling. In fact he persuaded me, and we actually made plans to do it.

But the continual lamentations of my mother hindered me from granting him the favor, or rather from receiving this boon at his hands. For when she perceived that I was meditating this step, she took me into her own private chamber, and, sitting near me on the bed where she had given birth to me, she shed torrents of tears, to which she added words yet more pitiable than her weeping, something like this:

"My child, it was not the will of heaven that I should long enjoy the benefit of your father's virtue. For his death soon followed the pangs which I endured at your birth, leaving you an orphan and me a widow before my time to face all the horrors of widowhood, which only those who have experienced them can fairly understand. For no words are adequate to describe the tempest-tossed condition of a young woman who, having but lately left her paternal home, and being inexperienced in business, is suddenly racked by an overwhelming sorrow, and compelled to support a load of care too great for her age and sex. She has to correct the laziness of servants, and to be on the watch for their mischief, to fight off the plots of relatives, to bear bravely the threats of those who collect the public taxes, and harshness in the imposition of rates.

"And if the departed one should have left a child, even if it be a girl, great anxiety will be caused to the mother, although free from much expense and fear: but a boy fills her with ten thousand alarms and many anxieties every day, to say nothing of the great expense which one is compelled to incur if she wishes to bring him up in a liberal way. None of these things, however, induced me to enter into a second marriage, or introduce a second husband into your father's house: but

I held on as I was, in the midst of the storm and uproar, and did not shun the iron furnace of widowhood. My foremost help indeed was the grace from above; but it was no small consolation to me under those terrible trials to look continually on your face and to preserve in you a living image of him who had gone, an image indeed which was a fairly exact likeness.

"On this account, even when you were an infant, and had not yet learned to speak, a time when children are the greatest delight to their parents, you gave me much comfort. Nor indeed can you complain that, although I bore my widowhood bravely, I diminished your patrimony, which I know has been the fate of many who have had the misfortune to be orphans. For, besides keeping the whole of it intact, I spared no expense that was needed to give you an honorable position, spending for this purpose some of my own fortune, and of my marriage dowry.

"Yet do not think that I say these things by way of reproaching you; only in return for all these benefits I beg one favor: do not plunge me into a second widowhood; nor revive the grief which is now laid to rest: wait for my death: it may be in a little while I shall depart. The young indeed look forward to a distant old age; but we who have grown old have nothing but death to wait for. When, then, you have laid my body in the ground, and mingled my bones with your father's, go on a long trip, and set sail on any sea you will. Then there will be no one to hinder you. But as long as my life lasts, be content to live with me. Do not, I beg you, oppose God in vain, involving me without cause, who have done you no wrong, in these great calamities. For if you have any reason to complain that I drag you into worldly cares, and force you to attend to business, do not be restrained by any reverence for the laws of nature, for training or custom, but fly from me as an enemy; but if, on the contrary, I do everything to provide leisure for your journey through this life, let this bond at least if nothing else keep you by me. For if you could say that ten thousand loved you, yet no one will let you have so much liberty, seeing there is no one who is equally anxious for your welfare."

These words, and more, my mother spoke to me, and I related them to that noble youth. But he, so far from being disheartened by these speeches, was the more urgent in making the same request as before.

So that was where we stood: he kept urging me, and I kept refusing my assent. And then suddenly we were both of us disturbed by a report that we were about to be advanced to the dignity of bishops.

As soon as I heard this rumor I was seized with alarm and perplexity: with alarm that I might be made captive against my will, and perplexity, inquiring as I often did whence any such idea concerning us could have entered the minds of these men; for looking to myself I found nothing worthy of such an honor.

But that noble youth came to me privately and conferred with me about these things as if with one who was ignorant of the rumor. Then he begged that we might in this instance also, as we always had in the past, shape our action and our counsels the same way: for he would readily follow me whichever course I might pursue, whether I attempted flight or submitted to be captured.

When I saw his eagerness, and considering that I should inflict a loss upon the whole body of the Church if, owing to my own weakness, I were to deprive the flock of Christ of a young man who was so good and so well qualified for the supervision of large numbers, I did not tell him what I had decided to do, although I had never before allowed any of my plans to be concealed from him. I now told him that it would be best to postpone our decision concerning this matter to another season, as it was not immediately pressing, and by so doing persuaded him to dismiss it from his thoughts. And at the same time, I encouraged him to hope that, if such a thing should ever happen to us, I should be of the same mind with him.

But after a short time, when one who was to ordain us arrived, I kept myself concealed, but Basil, ignorant of this, was taken away on another pretext, and made to take the yoke, hoping from the promises I had made to him that I should certainly follow—or rather supposing that he was following me. For some of those who were present, seeing that he resented being seized, deceived him by exclaiming how strange it was that one who was generally reputed to be the more hot-tempered (meaning me), had yielded very mildly to the judgment of the Fathers, whereas he, who was reckoned a much wiser and milder kind of man, had shown himself hotheaded and conceited, being unruly, restive, and contradictory.

Having yielded to these remonstrances, and afterwards having learned that I had escaped capture, he came to me in deep dejection, sat down near me and tried to speak, but was hindered by distress of mind and inability to express in words the violence to which he had been subjected. No sooner had he opened his mouth than he was prevented from utterance by grief cutting short his words before they could pass his lips.

Seeing, then, his tearful and agitated condition, and knowing as I did the cause, I laughed for joy, and, seizing his right hand, I forced a kiss on him, and praised God that my plan had ended so successfully, as I had always prayed it might. But when he saw that I was delighted and beaming with joy, and understood that he had been deceived by me, he was yet more vexed and distressed.

And when he had recovered a little from this agitation of mind, he began:

Basil. If you have rejected the part allotted to you, and have no further regard for me (I really don't know why), you ought at least to consider your own reputation; but as it is you have opened the mouths of all, and the world is saying that you have declined this ministry through love of vainglory, and there is no one who will deliver you from this accusation.

As for me, I cannot bear to go into the marketplace; there are so many who come up to me and reproach me every day. For, when they see me anywhere in the city, all my intimate friends take me aside, and cast the greater part of the blame upon me. 'You knew what he was planning,' they say, 'for none of his affairs could be kept secret from you. So you should not have concealed it, but ought to have told us about it, and we'd have had no trouble making some plan for capturing him.'

But I am too much ashamed and abashed to tell them that I did not know you had long been plotting this trick. I'm afraid they might say that our friendship was a mere pretense. For even if it is so, as indeed it is—nor would you yourself deny it after what you have done to me—yet it is well to hide our misfortune from the outside world, and persons who entertain but a moderate opinion of us. I shrink from telling them the truth, and how things really stand with us, and I am compelled in the future to keep silence, and look down on the ground, and turn away to avoid anyone I meet. For if I escape the condemnation on the former charge, I am forced to undergo judgment for speaking falsehood. For they will never believe me when I say that you counted Basil among those who are not permitted to know your secret affairs.

Of this, however, I will not take much account, since it has seemed agreeable to you, but how shall we endure the future disgrace? For some accuse you of arrogance, others of vainglory: while those who are our more merciful accusers, lay both these offenses to our charge, and add that we have insulted those who did us honor, although had they experienced even greater indignity it would only have served them right for passing over so many and such distinguished men and advancing mere youths, who were only yesterday immersed in the interests of this world, to such a dignity as they never have dreamed of obtaining, in order that they may for a brief time knit the eyebrows, wear dark clothes, and put on a grave face. People who have carefully disciplined themselves from the dawn of manhood to extreme old age are now to be placed under the government of youths who have not even heard the laws that should regulate their administration of this office. I am constantly assailed by persons who say such things and worse, and I have no idea how to reply to them; but I pray you tell me: for I do not suppose that you took to flight and incurred such hatred from such distinguished men without cause or consideration, but that your decision was made with reasoning and circumspection: from which also I suppose that you have some argument ready for your defense.

Tell me, then, whether there is any fair excuse which I can make to those who accuse us.

I'm not asking for anything in return for the wrong you've done to me, or for the deceit or treachery you have practiced, or for all I've done for you in the past. For I placed my very life in your hands, so to speak, yet you have treated me with as much guile as if it had been your business to guard yourself against an enemy. If you knew that this decision of ours would be a good thing, you shouldn't have avoided the gain yourself: and on the other hand if you thought it was a bad thing, you should have saved me from the loss, too, since you always said that you esteemed me more than everyone else. But you have done everything to make me fall into the snare. And you had no need of guile and hypocrisy in dealing with one who has always shown the utmost sincerity and candor in speech and action towards you.

Nevertheless, as I said, I'm not accusing you of any of these things now, or reproaching you for the lonely position in which you have placed me by breaking off those conferences that often gave us so much pleasure and profit. No, all these things I pass by, and bear in silence and meekness, not that you have acted meekly in transgressing against me, but because from the day that I cherished your friendship I laid it down as a rule for myself, that whatever sorrow you might cause me I would never force you to apologize for it. For you know yourself that you have inflicted no small loss on me—at least if you remember what we were always saying ourselves, and the outside world also said concerning us, that it was a great gain for us to be of one mind and be guarded by each other's friendship. In fact everyone said that our agreement would bring no small advantage to many besides ourselves.

Now, for myself, I could never tell how it could be of advantage to others. But I did say that we should at least derive this benefit from it: that those who wished to contend with us would find us difficult to master. And I never ceased reminding you of these things: saying the age is a cruel one, and designing men are many, genuine love is no more, and the deadly pest of envy has crept into its place: we walk in the midst of snares, and on the edge of battlements; those who are ready to rejoice in our misfortunes, if any should befall us, are many and beset us from many quarters: and on the other hand there is no one to condole with us, or at least the number of such may be easily counted. Beware that we do not by separation incur much ridicule, and damage worse than ridicule. Brother aided by brother is like a strong city, and well-fortified kingdom. Do not dissolve this genuine intimacy or break down the fortress.

I was always saying things like these, and more besides—not that I ever suspected anything of this kind, of course, but supposing you to be entirely sound in your relation towards me, I did it as an extra precaution, wishing to preserve in health one who was already sound. But it seems I didn't realize I was administering medicines to a sick man! And even so I have not been fortunate enough to do any good and have gained nothing by my excess of forethought.

For having totally thrown away all these considerations, without giving them a thought, you have turned me adrift like a ship with no ballast on an unknown ocean, taking no heed of those fierce billows which I must encounter. Now, if it should ever be my lot to undergo calumny, or mockery, or any other kind of insult or menace—and things like that happen all the time—to whom shall I fly for refuge? to whom shall I tell my distress? Who will be willing to help me and drive back my assailants and put a stop to their assaults? Who will console me and prepare me to bear the coarse ribaldry which may yet be in store for me?

There is no one, since you stand aloof from this terrible strife, and cannot even hear my cry.

Do you see, then, what mischief you have wrought? Now that you have dealt the blow, do you perceive what a deadly wound you have inflicted? But let all this pass: for it is impossible to undo the past, or to find a path through pathless difficulties. What shall I say to the outside world? What defense shall I make to their accusations?

Chrysostom. Be of good cheer, for I am not only ready to answer for myself in these matters, but I will also endeavor as well as I am able to render an account of the ones you have not held against me. Indeed, if you like, I will make them the starting point of my defense. For it would be a strange piece of stupidity on my part if, thinking only of praise from the outside public, and doing my best to silence their accusations, I were unable to convince my dearest of all friends that I am not wronging him, and were to treat him with indifference greater than the zeal which he has displayed on my behalf, treating me with such forbearance as even to refrain from accusing me of the wrongs which he says he has suffered from me, and putting his own interests out of the question in consideration for mine.

All right, since I've decided to set out on the sea of apology—what is the wrong that I have done you? Is it that I misled you and concealed my purpose? Yet I did it for the benefit of you, who were deceived, and of those to whom I surrendered you by means of this deceit. For if the evil of deception is absolute, and it is never right to make use of it, I am prepared to pay any penalty you please—or rather, as you will never endure to inflict punishment upon me, I shall subject myself to the same condemnation that is pronounced by judges on evil-doers when their accusers have convicted them. But if the thing is not always harmful, but becomes good or bad according to the intention of those who practice it, you must stop complaining of deceit, and prove that it has been devised against you for a bad purpose; and as long as this proof is lacking it would only be fair for those who wish to conduct themselves prudently not only to abstain from reproaches and accusation, but even to give a friendly reception to the deceiver.

For a well-timed deception, undertaken with an upright intention, has such advantages, that many persons have often had to undergo punishment for abstaining from fraud. And if you investigate the history of generals who have enjoyed the highest reputation from the earliest ages, you will find that most of their triumphs were achieved by stratagem, and that such are more highly commended than those who conquer in open fight. They use up more money and men in their campaigns, so that they gain nothing by the victory, but suffer just as much distress as those who have been defeated, both in the sacrifice of troops and the exhaustion of funds. Besides which, they are not even permitted to enjoy all the glory of the victory. A good bit of it goes to those who have fallen, because in spirit they were victorious, their defeat was only a bodily one: so that had it been possible for them not to fall when they were wounded, and death had not come and put the finishing stroke to their labors, there would have been no end of their prowess. But one who has been able to gain the victory by stratagem involves the enemy in ridicule as well as disaster. Again, in a victory in open fighting, both sides are equally honored for valor, whereas in this case they do not equally obtain those which are bestowed on wisdom, but the prize falls entirely to the victors. And, just as important, they preserve the joy of the victory for the state unalloyed. For abundance of resources and multitudes of men are not like mental powers. Resources and men get used up in war, and fail those who possess them, whereas it is the nature of wisdom to increase the more it is exercised.

And deceit is sometimes necessary not in war only, but also in peace—not merely in reference to the affairs of the state, but also in private life, in the dealings of husband with wife and wife with husband, son with father, friend with friend, and also children with a parent. For the daughter of Saul would not have been able to rescue her husband out of Saul's hands except by deceiving her father (see 1 Sam 19:11–17). And her brother, wishing to save him whom she had rescued when he was again in danger, made use of the same weapon as the wife (see 1 Sam 20:24–29).

Basil. But none of these cases apply to me: for I am not an enemy, and I am not one of those who are striving to injure you, but quite the contrary. I entrusted all my interests to your judgment, and always followed it whenever you asked me to.

Chrysostom. But, my admirable and excellent Sir, this is the very reason why I took the precaution of saying that it was a good thing to employ this kind of deceit, not only in war, and in dealing with enemies, but also in peace, and in dealing with our dearest friends. Here is a proof that it is beneficial not only to the deceivers, but also to those who are deceived: if you go to any of the physicians and ask them how they relieve their patients from disease, they will tell you that they do not depend upon their professional skill alone, but sometimes lead the sick to health by using deceit, and mixing its help with their art. For when the patient's stubbornness and the obstinacy of the complaint baffle the counsels of the physicians, it is then necessary to put on the mask of deceit in order that, as on the stage, they may be able to hide what really takes place.

But, if you like, I will tell you one example out of many that I have heard of a stratagem being contrived by the sons of the healing art. A man was once suddenly attacked by a fever of great severity; the burning heat increased, and the patient rejected the remedies which could have reduced it and craved for a drink of pure wine, passionately begging everyone who approached to give it him and enable him to satiate this deadly craving—I say deadly, for if anyone had gratified this request he would not only have exacerbated the fever, but also have driven the unhappy man frantic. Professional skill was baffled. The doctors were at their wit's end. All their work seemed to be for nothing. Then stratagem stepped in and saved the day.

Here's what happened: the physician took a pottery cup brought straight out of the furnace, and having steeped it in wine, then drew it out empty, filled it with water, and, having ordered the chamber where the sick man lay to be darkened with curtains that the light might not reveal the trick, he gave it him to drink, pretending that it was filled with undiluted wine. The man was deceived by the smell before he had taken it in his hands, so he did not wait to examine what was given him. Convinced by the odor, and deceived by the darkness, he eagerly gulped down the drink, and being satisfied with it immediately shook off the feeling of suffocation and escaped the imminent peril.

Do you see the advantage of deceit? And if anyone were to count up all the tricks of physicians, the list would run on forever.

And not only those who heal the body but those also who attend to the diseases of the soul may be found continually making use of this remedy. Thus the blessed Paul attracted those multitudes of Jews (see Acts 21:15-26). With this purpose he circumcised Timothy (Acts 16:3), although he warned the Galatians in his letter that Christ would not profit those who were circumcised (Gal 5:2). For this cause he submitted to the law, although he reckoned the righteousness which came from the law but loss after receiving the faith in Christ (Phil 3:7).

So deceit is very useful, as long as it is not done maliciously. In fact action of this kind ought not to be called deceit, but rather a kind of good management, cleverness and skill, capable of finding out ways where resources fail, and making up for the defects of the mind. For I would not call Phinehas a murderer, although he slew two human beings with one stroke (Num 25:7), nor yet Elias after the slaughter of the 100 soldiers and the captain (2 Kgs 1:9-12) and the torrents of blood which he caused to be shed by the destruction of those who sacrificed to devils (1 Kgs 18:34).

For if we were to concede this, and to examine the bare deeds in themselves apart from the intention of the doers, one might if he pleased judge Abraham guilty of child-murder (Gen 22) and accuse his grandson and his descendant of wickedness and guile. For the one got possession of the birthright (Gen 27), and the other transferred the wealth of the Egyptians to the host of the Israelites (Exod 11:2). But this is not true! Away with the audacious thought! For we not only acquit them of blame, but also admire them because of these things, since even God commended them for the same. For that man would fairly deserve to be called a deceiver who made an unrighteous use of the practice, not one who did so with a salutary purpose. And often it is necessary to deceive, and to do the greatest benefits by means of this device, whereas he who has gone by a straight course has done great mischief to the person whom he has not deceived.

Well, I might go on proving that it is possible to use deceit for a good purpose—or rather that we should not call it deceit in such a case, but a kind of admirably good management. But since I've already said enough to demonstrate it, it would be tiresome and annoying for me to go on. And now it will remain for you to prove whether I have not employed this art to your advantage.

Basil. And what kind of advantage have I gained from this piece of good management, or wise policy, or whatever you want to call it, that will persuade me that I have not been deceived by you?

Chrysostom. But what advantage could be greater than to be seen doing the things that Christ with his own lips declared to be proofs of love to himself? (See John 21:15–17.) For addressing the leader of the Apostles he said, "Peter, do you love me?" and when he confessed that he did, the Lord added, "If you love me, tend my sheep." The Master did not ask the disciple if he loved him to get information. He penetrates the hearts of all men. No, it was in order to teach us how great an interest he takes in the superintendence of these sheep.

Since this is clear, it will likewise be obvious that a great and unspeakable reward will be reserved for one whose labors are concerned with these sheep, upon which Christ places such a high value. For when we see any one bestowing care upon members of our household, or upon our flocks, we count his zeal for them as a sign of love towards ourselves. Yet you can buy all these things for money. Think how great the gift will be, then, for those who tend the flock Christ purchased, not with money or anything of that kind, but by his own death, giving his own blood as the price of the herd! . . .

Now, do you still insist that you were not rightly deceived, when you are about to superintend the things which belong to God, and are doing that which, when Peter did, the Lord said he should be able to surpass the rest of the Apostles? For his words were, "Peter, do you love me more than these?" Yet he might have said to him, "If you love me, practice fasting, sleeping on the ground, and prolonged vigils, defend the wronged, be as a father to orphans, and supply the place of a husband to their mother."

Now Chrysostom talks about how the sins of the priest can be mortal dangers to his flock. In particular, he warns against the sin of anger. But Basil knows that his friend John doesn't erupt in uncontrolled rages.

Basil: I will not put up with this irony of yours any longer. Everyone knows you don't have this trouble.

Chrysostom: Why then, my good friend, do you wish to bring me near the bonfire, and to provoke the wild beast when he is tranquil? Are you not aware that I have achieved this condition, not by any innate virtue, but by my love of retirement? When someone like that remains contented by himself, or only associates with one or two friends, he can escape the fire that arises from this passion—but not if he has plunged into the abyss of all these cares. Then he drags not only himself but many others with him to the brink of destruction and renders them more indifferent to all consideration for mildness. Most people who are governed tend to regard the manners of those who govern as a kind of model type, and to assimilate themselves to them. How then could anyone put a stop to their fury when he is swelling himself with rage? And who among the multitude would straightaway desire to become moderate when he sees the ruler irritable? For it is quite impossible for the defects of priests to be concealed, but even trifling ones quickly become obvious.

Chrysostom goes on to show, at great length and in great detail, how many dangers a priest has to worry about. He congratulates himself on escaping these dangers—and he seems quite surprised to find that Basil isn't consoled at all.

Rather self-centeredly, Chrysostom can't imagine any reason for distress when he himself doesn't have these things to worry about.

But why do you sigh? Why weep? For my case does not now call for wailing, but for joy and gladness.

Basil. But not *my* case! My case calls for countless lamentations. I can hardly comprehend yet how much evil you've brought me into. I came to you to ask what excuse I should make on your behalf to those who find fault with you, but you send me back with a different problem! Now I'm not worried about what excuses to give them on your behalf, but what excuse to make to God for myself and my own faults. But I beg you, and implore you, if you care at all about my welfare, if there is any encouragement in Christ, any incentive of love, any affection and sympathy (see Phil 2:1)—for you know that yourself above all brought me into this danger—stretch out your hand, both saying and doing what is able to restore me. Do not have the heart to leave me for the briefest moment, but now rather than before let me pass my life with you.

Chrysostom. [I smiled and said,] How can I help? What can I do for you when you carry so great a burden of office? But since this is pleasant to you, take courage, dear soul, for at any time at which it is possible for you to have leisure amid your own cares, I will come and will comfort you, and nothing shall be wanting of what is in my power.

On this, he stood up, weeping even more. But I embraced him and kissed his head, and then led him forth, exhorting him to bear his lot bravely. "For I believe," I said, "that through Christ who has called you, and set you over his own sheep, you will obtain such assurance from this ministry as to receive me also, if I am in danger at the last day, into your everlasting tabernacle."

—John Chrysostom, *On the Priesthood* 1.1–8; 6.13

Was Chrysostom really as clueless as he makes himself come across here? At this distance, it's hard to tell. But we should remember two things. First, he himself was the one who decided to end the dialogue with his friend Basil feeling even worse, not consoled. Second, Chrysostom did in fact become a priest and then a bishop. He was already a priest when he wrote this dialogue, and arguably more famous than the bishop of Antioch who was technically his superior. A few years later he was made patriarch of Constantinople—and a few years after that he died in exile, having made the common people love him but the upper classes hate him.

Maybe we're meant to see Chrysostom as the naive and arrogant young man he seems to be in this dialogue. Maybe we're meant to realize that all the dangers he congratulates himself on escaping were indeed piling up on him now. And maybe we're meant to imagine him thinking, "If I'd known then what I know today . . . "

THE PARADOX OF FRIENDSHIP

What is real friendship? It's a paradox, says Chrysostom. You never want to be in your friend's debt: you always want to do more for him than he does for you. At the same time, you want him to have the same feeling, because you know it will give him joy to feel that way.

Does this seem hard to understand? Perhaps it's because the paradox can only be resolved in heaven, where love is perfect.

Anyone who loves ought to love so much that if he were asked even for his soul, and it were possible, he would not refuse it. No—I don't mean if he were asked: I should say, so that he would even run to present him with the gift.

For nothing, nothing can be sweeter than such love; nothing will fall out there that is grievous. Truly, "a faithful friend is an elixir of life" (Sir 6:16). Truly, "a faithful friend is a sturdy shelter" (Sir 6:14). For what will a genuine friend not do? What pleasure will he not give us? What benefit? What security? Though you should name infinite treasures, none of them is comparable to a genuine friend.

And first let us speak of the great delight of friendship itself. A friend rejoices at seeing his friend and swells up with joy. He is knit to him with a union of soul that gives him unspeakable pleasure. And if he only thinks of his friend, he is roused in mind and transported.

I speak of genuine friends, men of one soul, who would even die for each other, who love fervently. Do not suppose that what I say is refuted when you think of those who barely love, who are table-companions, mere nominal friends. Anyone who has a friend of the kind I speak of knows that what I say is true. Even if you see your friend every day, it is not enough. You pray for your friend the same things you pray for yourself. I know someone who, calling upon holy men in behalf of his friend, asked them to pray first for him, and then for himself.

So dear a thing is a good friend, that times and places are loved on his account. For as bodies that are luminous spread their radiance to the neighboring places, so also friends leave a grace of their own in the places to which they have come. And often in the absence of friends, as we have stood on those places, we have wept, and remembering the days which we passed together, have sighed.

It is not possible to say in words how great a pleasure it is to be with friends. Only those who have experience can know. From a friend we may both ask a favor and receive one without suspicion. When they ask us to do something for them, then we feel indebted to them; but when they are slow to do this, then we are sorrowful. We have nothing that is not theirs. Often, though we despise all things here, on their account we are not willing to leave; and we long for them more than we long for the light.

In fact it really is true: a friend is more to be longed for than the light. I mean a real friend. And wonder not: for it were better for us that the sun should be extinguished, than that we should be deprived of friends; better to live in darkness, than to be without friends. And I will tell you why: because many who see the sun are in darkness, but people who have many friends can never be in tribulation. I mean spiritual friends, who prefer nothing to friendship. Paul was that kind of friend: he would willingly have given his own soul, even though not asked, nay would have plunged into hell for them. We ought to love with an ardent disposition like that.

I wish to give you an example of friendship. Friends—that is, friends according to Christ—surpass fathers and sons. For tell me not of friends of the present day, since this good thing also has passed away with others. But consider, in the time of the Apostles, I speak not of the chief men, but of the believers themselves generally; "all," he says, "were of one heart and soul, and not one of them said that anything of the things which he possessed was his own . . . and distribution was made to each as any had need" (Acts 4:32–35). Back then there were no such words as "mine" and "yours." This is friendship: that a man should not consider his goods his own, but his neighbor's, that his possessions belong to another; that he should be as careful of his friend's soul, as of his own; and the friend likewise.

And where is it possible, somebody says, that someone like that should be found? You say that because we have not the will—for it *is* possible. If it were not possible, Christ would not have commanded it; he would not have talked about love so much.

A great thing is friendship. No one can teach you and no one can tell you how great it is: you must experience it for yourself. Lack of friendship is what has caused the heresies. This makes the Greeks into Greeks. Whoever loves does not wish to command or to rule but is rather thankful to be ruled and commanded. He would rather do a favor than receive one, because he is not happy until he has a chance to demonstrate his love. He is gratified less when good is done to him than when he is doing good. For he wishes to oblige, rather than to be indebted to someone; or rather he wishes both to be indebted to him and to have him his debtor at the same time. And he wishes both to bestow favors, and not to seem to bestow them, but himself to be the debtor.

That may have been a little hard to understand. The one who loves wishes to be the first in bestowing benefits, but not to *seem* to be the first, but to be returning a kindness. This is what God has done for us. He decided to give his own Son for us; but, so that he might not seem to bestow a favor, but to be indebted to us, he commanded Abraham to offer his son, so that, while doing a great kindness, he might seem to do nothing great.

In fact, when there is no love, our very kindnesses seem to be rebukes, and we exaggerate little ones. But when there is love, we both conceal them and wish to make the great appear small, that we may not seem to have our friend for a debtor, but ourselves to be debtors to him, in having him our debtor.

I know most of you still don't understand what I'm saying, and the reason is that I am speaking of a thing that exists now in heaven. It's as if I were speaking of some plant growing in India, of which no one had ever had any experience: no speech would tell you what it was really like, though I should speak ten thousand words. In the same way, whatever I say now I say in vain, for no one will be able to understand me. This is a plant that is planted in heaven, having for its branches not heavy-clustered pearls, but a virtuous life, much more acceptable than they.

What pleasure would you speak of, foul or honorable? The pleasure of friendship excels them all, though you should speak of the sweetness of honey. For that satiates, but a friend never does, so long as he is a friend. In fact the desire of him rather increases, and such pleasure never admits of satiety. And a friend is sweeter than the present life. Many therefore after the death of their friends have not wished to live any longer. With a friend one would bear even banishment; but without a friend would not choose to inhabit even his own country. With a friend even poverty is tolerable, but without him both health and riches are intolerable. He has another self. I find myself in difficulty, because I cannot give you an example. If I could, you would see that what has been said is much less than it ought to be.

And these things indeed are so here. But from God the reward of friendship is so great, that it cannot be expressed. As a reward he gives us that we may love one another—the very thing for which we owe a reward. Pray, he says, and receive a reward, for that for which we owe a reward, because we ask for good things. For that which you ask, he says, receive a reward. Fast, and receive a reward. Be virtuous, and receive a reward, though really you ought to give *him* a reward. But fathers, when they have made their children virtuous, then give them a reward besides that; for the fathers are debtors, because the children have given them a pleasure. God acts the same way. Receive a reward, he says, if you are virtuous, for you delight your Father, and for this I owe you a reward. But if you are evil, not so: for you provoke him that begot you.

Let us not then provoke God, but let us delight him, so that we may obtain the kingdom of Heaven, in Christ Jesus our Lord, to whom be the glory and the strength, world without end. Amen.

—John Chrysostom, Homilies on First Thessalonians 2

REAL FRIENDSHIP TAKES AWAY A HOST OF SINS

Covetousness, slander, arrogance, falsehood—all these cannot continue where real friendship exists, says Chrysostom. The example of David and Jonathan from the Old Testament shows how friendship overcomes every obstacle and pushes us toward virtue.

Where there is love, all evils are removed. There is no love of money, the root of evil, there is no self-love: there is no boasting—for why should one boast over his friend? Nothing makes us so humble as love. We perform the duties of servants to our friends and are not ashamed; we are even thankful for the opportunity of serving them. We do not spare our property and often not our persons; for sometimes we must face dangers for someone we love.

There is no envy, no calumny, where there is genuine love. We not only do not slander our friends, but we stop the mouth of slanderers. All is gentleness and mildness. Not a trace of strife and contention appears. Everything breathes peace. For "Love," it is said, "is the fulfilling of the law" (Rom 13:10). There is nothing offensive with it. How can that be? Because where love exists, all the sins of covetousness, rapine, slander, arrogance, perjury, and falsehood are done away. People perjure themselves in order to rob, but no one would rob someone he loved, but would rather give him his own possessions—and feel more grateful than if he had received from him.

You know this, all you who have friends—I mean real friends, not friends in name only, but friends who really love the way we ought to love, friends who are really linked to another. And let those who are ignorant of it learn from those who know.

Now I will cite you from the Scriptures a wonderful instance of friendship. Jonathan, the son of Saul, loved David, and his soul was so knit to him, that David in mourning over him says, "Your love to me was wonderful, passing the love of women" (2 Sam 1:26) and "You were wounded unto death" (cf. 2 Sam 1:25). What then? Did he envy David? Not at all, though he had great reason.

What reason? By the events he could see that the kingdom would pass from himself to David, yet he felt no envy at all. He did not say, "This is the one who is depriving me of my paternal kingdom," but he favored David's gaining the rule; and for the sake of his friend he spared not his father. Yet no one can call him a parricide, for he did not injure his father, but just restrained his unjust attempts. He rather spared than injured him. He did not permit him to proceed to an unjust murder.

He was many times willing even to die for his friend, and far from accusing him, he restrained even his father's accusation. Instead of envying, he joined in obtaining the kingdom for him. Why do I speak of wealth? He even sacrificed his own life for him. For the sake of his friend, he did not even stand in awe of his father, since his father entertained unjust designs, but his conscience was free from all such designs. Thus justice was joined with friendship.

Such then was Jonathan. Let us now consider David. He had no opportunity of returning the favor, for his benefactor was taken away before the reign of David, and slain before he whom he had served came to his kingdom. What then? As far as it was allowed him and left in his power, let us see how that righteous man manifested his friendship. "Very pleasant," he says, "have you been to me, Jonathan; you were wounded unto death" (cf. 2 Sam 1:25–26). Is this all? This indeed was no slight tribute, but he also frequently rescued Jonathan's son and grandson from danger, in remembrance of the kindness of the father, and he continued to support and protect his children, as he would have done those of his own son. Such friendship I would wish all to entertain both towards the living and the dead.

—John Chrysostom, Homily 7 on Second Timothy

8.

THEODORET

THEODORET ended up on the wrong side of some of the most convoluted controversies in Church history. He made an enemy of St. Cyril of Alexandria, who could hold a grudge for centuries, and he sided with Nestorius until he was finally persuaded to condemn Nestorius at the Council of Chalcedon. So for much of the Church, Theodoret occupies an iffy middle ground: one of the Fathers, but not one of the *reliable* ones.

To be fair to him, though, Theodoret never wanted any of that excitement. His is another one of those "They Made Me a Bishop" stories, where the poor man tries his best not to be a bishop, only to discover that not wanting to be a bishop is one of the primary qualifications for being a bishop. He also did more than almost anyone else to make peace between the sides in the Nestorian controversy. And if he couldn't get along with Cyril—well, getting along with a steamroller like Cyril was a tough job under the best circumstances. "At last and with difficulty the villain has gone!" he wrote to another bishop when he heard that Cyril had died. "The good and the gentle pass away all too soon; the bad prolong their life for years. . . . Great care must then be taken, and it is especially your holiness's business to undertake this duty, to tell the guild of undertakers to lay a very big and heavy stone upon his grave, for fear he should come back again, and show his fickle mind once more."[1]

That was not a very friendly way to say farewell, we must admit.

But his many successful peacemaking efforts show that Theodoret had a great capacity for friendship. And he has left us some delightful little sayings about friendship in his letters. These may atone for the nasty things he said about St. Cyril.

Sincere friendships are neither dissolved by distance nor weakened by time. Time indeed inflicts indignities on our bodies, spoils them of the bloom of their beauty, and brings on old age; but of friendship he makes the beauty yet more blooming, ever kindling its fire to greater warmth and brightness.

So, separated as I am from your magnificence by many a day's march, pricked by the goad of friendship, I send you this greeting by letter . . .

—Theodoret, Letter 59

Those who try to observe the laws of friendship increase the strength of its love, and, blowing sparks into a flame, kindle a greater warmth of affection, while all who are fired by it strive to surpass one another in love.

—Theodoret, Letter 61

[1] Theodoret, Letter 180.

I perceive that it is with reason that I am well disposed to your reverences, for I have been assured by your kindly letter that my affection was returned. I have many reasons for this affection of mine towards you. First of all, there is the fact that your father, that great and apostolic man, was my father too. Secondly I look upon that truly religious bishop, who now rules your church, as I might on a brother both in blood and in sympathy. Thirdly there is the near neighborhood of our cities, and fourthly that we meet one another frequently, which naturally begets friendship and increases it when it is begotten.

—Theodoret, Letter 75

True friendship is strengthened by being together. But separation cannot break it, for its bonds are strong. This truth might easily be shown by many other examples, but it is enough for us to verify what I say by our own case. There are many things between you and me—mountains, cities, and the sea—yet nothing has destroyed my recollection of your excellency.

—Theodoret, Letter 76

9.

JOHN CASSIAN

St. John Cassian lived at the same time as Augustine, Chrysostom, and Jerome. It's staggering to think how much talent the Church produced in their time—all the more staggering because the rest of the world seemed to be in a mess. The Roman Empire was busy declining and falling at a rapid pace. Barbarians were at the gates.

Nevertheless, John Cassian managed to be equally familiar with the East and the West. He was probably born somewhere in the middle, but he spent some of his youth in the Holy Land, and then many years as a monk in Egypt. After that he went to Constantinople, where he got to know St. John Chrysostom very well. When Chrysostom was exiled, Cassian went to Rome to plead Chrysostom's case with the pope. (The pope came down firmly on Chrysostom's side, which did him no good at all.) Eventually he ended up in Marseille, where he set up a monastery modeled after the ones he had known in Egypt, thus becoming one of the founders of Western monasticism.

His *Conferences* supposedly record conversations with the wise elders at his Egyptian monastery. In Conference 16, the subject of friendship comes up—specifically, friendship between monks. In this case, the two young monks are John himself and his friend Germanus.

The blessed Joseph, whose instructions and precepts you are about to hear, and who was one of the three whom we mentioned in the first Conference, belonged to a most illustrious family, and was the chief man of his city in Egypt, which was named Thmuis. Thus he was carefully trained in the eloquence of Greece as well as Egypt, so that he could talk admirably with us or with those who were utterly ignorant of Egyptian, not through an interpreter (as the others did), but in his own person.

And when he found that we were anxious for instruction from him, he first inquired whether we were biological brothers, and when he heard that we were united in a tie of spiritual and not carnal brotherhood, and that from the first beginning of our renunciation of the world we had always been joined together in an unbroken bond as well in our travels, which we had both undertaken for the sake of spiritual service, as also in the pursuits of the monastery, he began his discourse as follows.

THE WRONG KIND OF FRIENDSHIP

Joseph. There are many kinds of friendship and companionship which unite men in very different ways in the bonds of love. A previous recommendation brings some together, first as acquaintances, and afterwards even as friends. In the case of others, some bargain or an agreement to give and take something has joined them in the bonds of love. Others are united in the chain of friendship by a similarity and union of business or science or art or study, by which even fierce souls become kindly disposed to each other. Even those in the forests and mountains who delight in robbery and revel in human bloodshed embrace and cherish the partners of their crimes.

But there is another kind of love, where the union is from the instincts of nature and the laws of relationships, by which those of the same tribe, wives and parents, and brothers and children are naturally preferred to others—a thing we find not only with mankind but also with all birds and beasts. At the prompting of a natural instinct they protect and defend their offspring and their young ones, so that often they are not afraid to expose themselves to danger and death for their sake. Indeed those kinds of beasts and serpents and birds, which are cut off and separated from all others by their intolerable ferocity or deadly poison, as basilisks, unicorns and vultures, though by their very look they are said to be dangerous to everyone, yet among themselves they remain peaceful and harmless owing to community of origin and fellow-feeling.

But all these kinds of love of which we have spoken are common both to the good and bad, and to beasts and serpents, so we see they certainly cannot last forever. Often separation of place interrupts and breaks them off, as well as forgetfulness from lapse of time, and the transaction of affairs and business and words. Since they are generally due to different kinds of connections—either of gain, or desires, or kinship, or business—so when any occasion for separation intervenes, they are broken off.

THE KIND OF FRIENDSHIP THAT CANNOT BE DISSOLVED

Now, among all these there is one kind of love that is indissoluble, where the union is owing not to the favor of a recommendation, or some great kindness or gifts, or the reason of some bargain, or the necessities of nature, but simply to similarity of virtue. This, I say, is what is broken by no chances, what no interval of time or space can sever or destroy, and what even death itself cannot part. This is true and unbroken love, which grows by means of the double perfection and goodness of friends, and which, when once its bonds have been entered, no difference of liking and no disturbing opposition of wishes can sever.

But we have known many set on this purpose, who though they had been joined together in companionship out of their burning love for Christ, yet could not maintain it continually and without a break, because although they relied on a good beginning for their friendship, yet they did not with one and the same zeal maintain the purpose on which they had entered. So there was between them a sort of love only for a while, for it was not maintained by the goodness of both alike, but by the patience of the one party. And so, although it is held to by the one with unwearied heroism, yet it is sure to be broken by the pettiness of the other.

For the infirmities of those who are somewhat cold in seeking the healthy condition of perfection, however patiently they may be borne by the strong, are yet not put up with by those who are weaker themselves. They have implanted within them causes of disturbance that do not allow them to be at ease—just as those who are affected by bodily weakness generally impute the delicacy of their stomach and weak health to the carelessness of their cooks and servants. However carefully their attendants may serve them, yet nevertheless they ascribe the grounds of their upset to those who are in good health, as they do not see that they are really due to the failure of their own health.

This, therefore, as we said, is the sure and indissoluble union of friendship, where the tie consists only in likeness in goodness. For the Lord makes men to be of one mind in a house. And therefore love can only continue undisturbed in those in whom there is but one purpose and mind to will and to refuse the same things. And if you also wish to keep this unbroken, you must be careful that having first got rid of your faults, you mortify your own desires, and with united zeal and purpose diligently fulfill that in which the prophet specially delights: "Behold, how good and pleasant it is when brothers dwell in unity!" (Ps 133:1). Which should be understood as unity of spirit rather than of place. It is of no use for those who differ in character and purpose to be united in one dwelling, nor is it a hindrance for those who are grounded on equal goodness to be separated by distance. For with God the union of character, not of place, joins brethren together in a common dwelling, nor can unruffled peace ever be maintained where difference of will appears.

LASTING FRIENDSHIP EXISTS ONLY AMONG THE PERFECT

Germanus. But how about this: if one party wants to do something he thinks is useful and profitable according to the mind of God, but the other does not give his consent, should it be done even against the wish of the brother, or should it be given up as he wants?

Joseph. This is why I said that the full and perfect grace of friendship can only last among those who are perfect and of equal goodness. Because they have the same mind and a common purpose, they never—well, hardly ever—disagree or differ in things that concern their progress in the spiritual life. But if they begin to get agitated with heated arguments, it is clear that they have never been at one in accordance with the rule I gave above.

But because no one can start from perfection except one who has begun from the very foundation, and your question is not about its greatness, but as to how you can attain to it, I think it well to explain to you, in a few words, the rule for it and the sort of path along which your steps should be directed, that you may be able more easily to secure the blessing of patience and peace.

HOW TO REACH THAT PERFECTION

So the first foundation of true friendship consists in contempt for worldly possessions and scorn for all things that we own. For it is utterly wrong and unjustifiable if, after we renounce the vanity of the world and all that is in it, we place more value on whatever miserable furniture remains than on what is most valuable—namely, the love of a brother.

The second is for each man to prune his own wishes so that he may not imagine himself to be a wise and experienced person, and so prefer his own opinions to those of his neighbor.

The third is for you to recognize that everything, even what you think is useful and necessary, must come after the blessing of love and peace.

The fourth is for you to realize that you should never be angry for any reason, good or bad.

The fifth is for you to try to cure any wrath that a brother may have conceived against you, however unreasonably, in the same way that you would cure your own, knowing that the vexation of another is just as bad for you as if you yourself were stirred against another, until you remove it, to the best of your ability, from your brother's mind.

The last is what is undoubtedly generally decisive in regard to all faults: namely, that you should realize daily that you are going to pass away from this world. When you realize this, it not only permits no vexation to linger in the heart, but it also represses all the motions of lusts and sins of all kinds. So whoever has got hold of this can neither suffer bitter wrath and discord nor be the cause of it. But when this fails, as soon as he who is jealous of love has little by little infused the poison of vexation in the hearts of friends, it is certain that owing to frequent quarrels love will gradually grow cool, and at some time or other he will part the hearts of the lovers, that have been for a long while exasperated.

Now, if you are walking along the course I just marked out, how can you ever differ from your friend? If you claim nothing for yourself, you entirely cut off the first cause of quarrel (which generally springs from trivial things and most unimportant matters), as you observe to the best of your power what we read in the Acts of the Apostles on the unity of believers: "Now the company of those who believed were of one heart and soul, and no one said that any of the things which he possessed was his own, but they had everything in common" (Acts 4:32).

Then how can any seeds of argument sprout from anyone who serves not his own but his brother's will, and becomes a follower of his Lord and Master, who speaking in the character of man which he had taken, said, "I have come down from heaven, not to do my own will, but the will of him who sent me"? (John 6:38). And how can anyone arouse any incitement to contention who has determined to trust not so much to his own judgment as to his brother's decision, on his own intelligence and meaning, in accordance with his will either approving or disapproving his discoveries, and fulfilling in the humility of a pious heart these words from the Gospel: "nevertheless, not as I will, but as you will" (Matt 26:39).

Or in what way will you allow anything that grieves your brother, if you think that nothing is more precious than the blessing of peace, and never forget these words of the Lord: "By this all men will know that you are my disciples, if you have love for one another" (John 13:35). For by this, as by a special mark, Christ willed that the flock of his sheep should be known in this world, and be separated from all others by this stamp, so to speak.

And on what grounds will you endure either to admit the rancor of vexation in yourself or for it to remain in another, if your firm decision is that there cannot be any good ground for anger, as it is dangerous and wrong, and that when your brother is angry with you he cannot pray, in just the same way as when you yourself are angry with your brother, as you always keep in a humble heart these words of our Lord and Savior:

"So if you are offering your gift at the altar, and there remember that your brother has something against you, leave your gift there before the altar and go; first be reconciled to your brother, and then come and offer your gift" (Matt 5:23–24).

It will be of no use for you to declare that you are not angry, and to believe that you are fulfilling the command that says, "do not let the sun go down on your anger" (Eph 4:25) and: "every one who is angry with his brother shall be liable to judgment" (Matt 5:22), if you are with obstinate heart disregarding the vexation of another which you could smooth down by kindness on your part. You will be punished just the same for violating the Lord's command. The same Lord who said that you should not be angry with another also said that you should not disregard the vexations of another. It makes no difference in the sight of God, "who desires all men to be saved" (1 Tim 2:4), whether you destroy yourself or someone else. The death of anyone is equally a loss to God. And at the same time, it is equally a gain to him to whom all destruction is delightful, whether it is acquired by your death or by the death of your brother.

Lastly, how can you hold onto even the least vexation with your brother, if you realize daily that he is going to depart from this world soon?

So, then, nothing should be put before love. And likewise, on the other hand, nothing should be put below rage and anger. You should give up everything, no matter how useful and necessary it may seem, so that disturbing anger may be avoided. And even all the things we think are unfortunate should be undertaken and endured, so that the calm of love and peace may be preserved unimpaired—because we should reckon nothing more damaging than anger and vexation, and nothing more advantageous than love.

WATCH OUT FOR DISCORD

For as our enemy separates brethren who are still weak and carnal by a sudden burst of rage on account of some trifling and earthly matter, so he sows the seeds of discord even between spiritual persons, on the ground of some difference of thoughts. This is where most of those arguments and fights about words that the Apostle condemns come from: our spiteful and malignant enemy uses them to sow discord between brethren who were of one mind. For these words of wise Solomon are true: "Hatred stirs up strife, but love covers all offenses" (Prov 10:12).

So, for the preservation of lasting and unbroken love, it is of no use to have removed the first ground of discord, which generally arises from frail and earthly things, or to have disregarded all carnal things, and to have permitted to our brethren an unrestricted share in everything which our needs require, unless we also cut off in the same way the second, which generally arises under the guise of spiritual feelings; and unless we gain in everything humble thoughts and harmonious wills.

DON'T TRUST YOUR OWN JUDGMENT

I remember that, when my youthful age suggested to me to cling to a partner, thoughts of this sort often mingled with our moral training and the Holy Scriptures, so that we imagined that nothing could be truer or more reasonable. But when we came together and began to produce our ideas, in the general discussion which was held, some things were first noted by the others as false and dangerous, and then presently were condemned and pronounced by common consent to be injurious; though before they had seemed to shine as if with a light infused by the devil, so that they would easily have caused discord, had not the charge of the Elders, observed like some divine oracle, restrained us from all strife—that charge, namely, in which they ordered (almost with the force of a law!) that neither of us should trust to his own judgments more than his brother's, if he wanted never to be deceived by the craft of the devil.

Yes, it has often been proved that what the Apostle says really does happen: "even Satan disguises himself as an angel of light" (2 Cor 11:14). He deceitfully sheds abroad a confusing and foul obscuration of the thoughts instead of the true light of knowledge. And unless these thoughts are received in a humble and gentle heart, and kept for the consideration of some more experienced brother or approved Elder, and when thoroughly sifted by their judgment, either rejected or admitted by us, we shall be sure to venerate in our thoughts an angel of darkness instead of an angel of light, and be struck with a grievous destruction.

It is impossible for anyone to avoid this injury who trusts in his own judgment, unless he becomes a lover and follower of true humility and with all contrition of heart fulfills what the Apostle chiefly prays for: "So if there is any encouragement in Christ, any incentive of love, any participation in the Spirit, any affection and sympathy, complete my joy by being of the same mind, having the same love, being in full accord and of one mind. Do nothing from selfishness or conceit, but in humility count others better than yourselves" (Phil 2:1–3). Prefer one another in honor, so that each may think more of the knowledge and holiness of his partner and hold that the better part of true discretion is to be found in the judgment of another rather than in your own.

Now, it often happens either by an illusion of the devil or by simple human error (by which everyone in this life is liable to be deceived) that one who is keener in intellect and more learned gets some wrong notion in his head, while one who is duller in wits and of less worth conceives the matter better and more truly. And therefore no one, however learned he may be, should persuade himself in his empty vanity that he cannot require conference with another.

For even if no deception of the devil blinds your judgment, yet you cannot avoid the noxious snares of pride and conceit. For who can arrogate this to himself without great danger, when the chosen vessel in whom, as he maintained, Christ himself spoke, declares that he went up to Jerusalem simply and solely for this reason, that he might in a secret discussion confer with his fellow Apostles on the Gospel which he preached to the Gentiles by the revelation and cooperation of the Lord?

By this we are shown not only that we should preserve unanimity and harmony by these precepts, but also that we need not fear any crafts of the devil opposing us, or snares of his illusions.

THE KINDS OF LOVE

Finally, so highly is the virtue of love praised that the blessed Apostle John declares that it not only belongs to God but that it *is* God, saying, "God is love, and he who abides in love abides in God, and God abides in him" (1 John 4:16). Love is such a divine thing that we find that what the Apostle says is plainly a living truth in us: "God's love has been poured into our hearts through the Holy Spirit which has been given to us" (Rom 5:5). It is the same thing as if he said that God is shed abroad in our hearts by the Holy Spirit who dwells in us: who also, when we do not know what we should pray for, "intercedes for us with sighs too deep for words. And he who searches the hearts of men knows what is the mind of the Spirit, because the Spirit intercedes for the saints according to the will of God" (Rom 8:26–27).

So it is possible for everyone to show that love which is called *agape*, of which the blessed Apostle says: "So then, as we have opportunity, let us do good to all men, and especially to those who are of the household of faith" (Gal 6:10). We should show this kind of love to everyone in general—so much so that we are actually commanded by our Lord to give it to our enemies, for he says, "Love your enemies" (Matt 5:44).

But real affection is shown to only a few, those who are united to us by similar dispositions or by a tie of goodness—though indeed affection seems to have many degrees of difference. For in one way we love our parents, in another our wives, in another our brothers, in another our children, and there is a wide difference in regard to the claims of these feelings of affection, nor is the love of parents towards their children always equal.

We see this in the case of the patriarch Jacob, who, though he was the father of twelve sons and loved them all with a father's love, yet loved Joseph with deeper affection, as Scripture clearly shows: "But when his brothers saw that their father loved him more than all his brothers, they hated him" (Gen 37:4). This does not seem to mean that his father, who was a good man, failed in greatly loving the rest of his children, but that in his affection he clung to this one more tenderly and indulgently, because he was a foreshadowing of the Lord.

Again, we see it very clearly in the case of John the Evangelist, where these words are used of him: "One of his disciples, whom Jesus loved" (John 13:23)—though certainly Jesus embraced all the other eleven, whom he had chosen in the same way, with his special love, which he shows by the witness of the Gospel where he says, "even as I have loved you, that you also love one another" (John 13:34); of whom elsewhere also it is said, "having loved his own who were in the world, he loved them to the end" (John 13:1). But this love of one in particular did not indicate any coldness in love for the rest of the disciples, but only a fuller and more abundant love towards the one, which his prerogative of virginity and the purity of his flesh bestowed upon him. And therefore it is marked by exceptional treatment, as being something more sublime, because no hateful comparison with others, but a richer grace of superabundant love singled it out.

Something of this sort too we have in the character of the bride in the Song of Songs, where she says, "he set in order charity in me" (Song 2:4, Douay-Rheims version). For this is true love set in order: while it hates no one, yet it loves some still more because they deserve it; and while it loves all in general, it singles out for itself some whom it may embrace with a special affection—and again, out of those who are the special and chief objects of its love, singles out some who are preferred to others in affection.

HIDING YOUR FEELINGS LEADS TO TROUBLE

On the other hand I know—and how I wish I did not know!—some of the brethren who are so hard and stubborn that, when they know that their own feelings are aroused against their brother, or that their brother's are against them, hide their annoyance, which is caused by indignation at the grievance of one or the other, by going off somewhere away from those whom they ought to smooth down by humbly making up to them and talking with them, and begin to sing some verses of the Psalms.

They think they are softening the bitter thoughts that have arisen in their heart, but in fact they increase by their insolent conduct what they could have got rid of at once if they had been willing to show more care and humility. For a well-timed expression of regret would cure their own feelings and soften their brother's heart. By that plan they nourish and cherish the sin of meanness or rather of pride, instead of stamping out all inducement to quarreling, and they forget the charge of the Lord which says that "every one who is angry with his brother shall be liable to judgment," and "if you are offering your gift at the altar, and there remember that your brother has something against you, leave your gift there before the altar and go; first be reconciled to your brother, and then come and offer your gift" (Matt 5:22–24).

Thus our Lord is so anxious that we should not disregard the vexation of another that he does not accept our offerings if our brother has anything against us. That is, he does not allow us to offer prayers to him until we quickly remove from his (our brother's) mind the vexation he feels—

whether he has any reason to feel it or not. For he does not say, "if your brother has a *true* ground for complaint against you, leave your gift there before the altar and go; first be reconciled to your brother"; but he says, "if you remember that your brother has something against you"—meaning if there is anything however trivial or small that makes your brother angry with you, and you suddenly happen to remember it, you must know that you should not offer the spiritual gift of your prayers until you have done something kind to remove the vexation from your brother's heart, whatever the reason for it may have been.

Now, if the words of the Gospel bid us make satisfaction to those who are angry for past and utterly trivial grounds of quarrel, and those that have arisen from the slightest causes, what will become of us wretches who with obstinate hypocrisy disregard more recent grounds of offense, and those of the utmost importance, and due to our own faults? What will happen if, puffed up with the devil's own pride and ashamed to humble ourselves, we deny that we are the cause of our brother's vexation? What will happen if, in a spirit of rebellion, we refuse to be subject to the Lord's commands, and insist that they never ought to be observed and can never be fulfilled? And so, as we make up our minds that he has commanded things that are impossible and unsuitable, we end up being, to use the Apostle's expression, not doers but judges of the law (see Jas 4:11).

Here is another thing that should bitterly grieve us. Some of the brethren may be angered by some reproachful words, and then they are besieged by the prayers of someone else who wants to calm them down. So when they hear that vexation ought not to be allowed or retained against a brother, according to what is written, "every one who is angry with his brother shall be liable to judgment," and "do not let the sun go down on your anger" (Eph 4:26), they instantly assert that if a heathen or one living in the world had said or done this, it rightly ought to be endured. But who could stand a brother who was accessory to so great a fault, or gave utterance to so insolent a reproach with his lips?

As if patience were to be shown only to unbelievers and blasphemers, and not to all in general! As if anger should be reckoned as bad when it is against a heathen, but good when it is against a brother!

No, certainly the stubborn rage of an angry soul brings about the same injury to oneself whoever may be the subject against whom it is aroused. But how terribly stubborn—senseless, too—is it for them, owing to the stupidity of their dull mind, not to be able to discern the meaning of these words! It is not said, "every one who is angry with a *stranger* shall be liable to judgment," which might perhaps, according to their interpretation, leave out those who are partners of our faith and life. No, the word of the Gospel most significantly expresses it by saying, "every one who is angry with his *brother* shall be liable to judgment." And so, though we ought according to the rule of truth to regard every man as a brother, yet in this passage one of the faithful and a partaker of our mode of life is denoted by the title of brother rather than a heathen.

WE MAY BE SINNING WHEN WE THINK WE'RE EXERCISING VIRTUE

But what about this? Sometimes we imagine that we are patient because, when provoked, we scorn to answer, but by sullen silence or scornful motions and gestures so mock at our angry brothers that by our silent looks we provoke them to anger more than angry reproaches would have excited them! Meanwhile we think that we are in no way guilty before God, because we have let nothing fall from our lips that could brand us or condemn us in the judgment of men.

As if in the sight of God mere words, and not mainly the will, was called in fault! As if only the actual deed of sin, and not also the wish and purpose, was reckoned as wrong! As if it would be asked in the judgment only what each one had done and not what he also *meant* to do!

For it is not only the character of the anger roused that is bad, but also the purpose of the man who provokes it. And therefore the true scrutiny of our judge will ask, not how the quarrel was stirred up, but by whose fault it arose. The purpose of the sin, and not the way in which the fault is committed must be taken into account.

For what does it matter whether a man kills a brother with a sword by himself, or drives him to death by some fraud, when it is clear that he is killed by his wiles and crime? As if it were enough not to have pushed a blind man down with one's own hand, though he is equally guilty who refused to save him, when it was in his power, when he had fallen and was on the point of tumbling into the ditch. Or as if he alone were guilty who had caught a man with the hand, and not also the one who had prepared and set the trap for him, or who would not set him free when he might have done so.

So then it is no good to hold one's tongue, if we impose silence upon ourselves so that by our silence we may do what would have been done by an outcry on our part, simulating certain gestures by which the one we ought to have cured may be made still more angry, while we are commended for all this, to his loss and damage. As if a man were not for this very reason the more guilty, because he tried to get glory for himself out of his brother's fall! For such a silence will be equally bad for both: while it increases the vexation in the heart of another, so it prevents it from being removed from one's own. Against such persons the prophet's curse is with good reason directed: "Woe to him who makes his neighbors drink of the cup of his wrath, and makes them drunk, to gaze on their shame! You will be sated with contempt instead of glory" (Hab 2:15–16). And this too which is said of such people by another: "For every brother will utterly supplant, and every friend will walk deceitfully. And a man shall mock his brother, and they will not speak the truth, for they have bent their tongue like a bow for lies and not for truth" (Jer 9:4–5).

But often a pretended patience excites someone to anger more keenly than words, and a spiteful silence exceeds the most awful insults in words, and the wounds of enemies are more easily borne than the deceitful blandishment of mockers, of which it is well said by the prophet, "his words were softer than oil, yet they were drawn swords": and else-where, "the words of the crafty are soft: but they strike in the belly": to which this also may be finely applied: "with his mouth each speaks peaceably to his neighbor, but in his heart he plans an ambush for him" (Jer 9:8). But with this it is really the deceiver who is deceived—for if a man prepares a net before his friend, it surrounds his own feet; and "May he who digs a pit for his neighbor fall into it" (Prov 26:27, Septuagint).

Lastly when a great multitude had come with swords and staves to take the Lord, none of the murderers of the author of our life stood forth as more cruel than the one who advanced before them all with a counterfeit respect and salutation and offered a kiss of feigned love. To him the Lord said, "Judas, would you betray the Son of man with a kiss?" (Luke 22:48). That is, the bitterness of your persecution and hatred has taken as a cloak the thing that expresses the sweetness of true love. More openly too and more energetically does he emphasize the force of this grief by the prophet, saying: "It is not an enemy who taunts me—then I could bear it; it is not an adversary who deals insolently with me—then I could hide from him. But it is you, my equal, my companion, my familiar friend. We used to hold sweet converse together; within God's house we walked in fellowship" (Ps 55:12–14).

There is also another evil sort of vexation that would not be worth mentioning if we did not know that it is allowed by some of the brethren. When they have been vexed or enraged, they actually abstain persistently from food, so that (and we cannot mention this without shame) those who, when they are calm, tell us that they cannot possibly put off their refreshment to the sixth or at most the ninth hour, when they are filled with vexation and rage do not feel fasts even for two days, and support themselves, when exhausted by such abstinence, by a surfeit of anger.

In this they are plainly guilty of the sin of sacrilege, as out of the devil's own rage they endure fasts which ought specially to be offered to God alone out of desire for humiliation of heart and purification from sin. It is much the same as if they were to offer prayers and sacrifices not to God but to devils, and so be worthy of hearing this rebuke of Moses: "They sacrificed to demons which were no gods, to gods they had never known" (Deut 32:17).

We are not ignorant also of another kind of insanity, which we find in some of the brethren under color of a false patience. For them it is not enough to have stirred up quarrels unless they incite them with irritating words so as to get themselves struck, and when they have been touched by the slightest blow, at once they offer another part of their body to be struck, as if in this way they could fulfill to perfection that command which says, "if any one strikes you on the right cheek, turn to him the other also" (Matt 5:39)—while they totally ignore the meaning and purpose of the passage. For they fancy that they are practicing evangelical patience through the sin of anger! But not only was it for the utter eradication of the sin of anger that retaliation and the irritation of strife was forbidden, but the command was actually given us to mitigate the wrath of the striker by the endurance of a double wrong.

CHRIST LOOKS AT THE MOTIVE, NOT JUST THE ACT

Germanus. How can we blame one who satisfies the command of the Gospel and not only does not retaliate, but is actually prepared to have a double wrong offered to him?

Joseph. As I said a little before, we must look not only at the thing that is done, but also at the character of the mind and the purpose of the doer. And therefore if you weigh with a careful scrutiny of heart what is done by each man and consider with what mind it is done or from what feeling it proceeds, you will see that the virtue of patience and gentleness cannot possibly be fulfilled in the opposite spirit, the spirit of impatience and rage.

Our Lord and Savior gave us a thorough lesson on the virtue of patience and gentleness. I mean that he taught us not only to profess it with our lips, but to store it up in the inmost recesses of the soul. He gave us this summary of evangelical perfection, saying, "if any one strikes you on the right cheek, turn to him the other also." Doubtless the right cheek is mentioned because another right cheek cannot be found except in the face of the inner man, so to speak. So by this he desires to remove all incitement to anger completely from the deepest recesses of the soul, meaning that if your external right cheek has received a blow from the striker, the inner man also humbly consenting may offer its right cheek to be struck, sympathizing with the suffering of the outward man, and in a way submitting and subjecting its own body to wrong from the striker, so that the inner man may not even silently be disturbed in itself at the blows of the outward man.

You see then that they are very far from evangelical perfection. The Gospel teaches that patience must be maintained, not in words but in inward tranquility of heart, and which bids us preserve it whatever evil happens, so that we may not only keep ourselves always from disturbing anger, but also by submitting to their injuries compel those who are disturbed by their own fault to become calm when they have had their fill of blows. Thus we overcome their rage by our gentleness.

And so also we shall fulfill these words of the Apostle: "Do not be overcome by evil, but overcome evil with good" (Rom 12:21). And it is quite clear that this cannot be fulfilled by those who utter words of gentleness and humility in such a spirit and rage that they not only fail to lessen the fire of wrath which has been kindled, but rather make it blaze up the more fiercely both in their own feelings and in those of their enraged brother.

But even if they *could* in some way keep calm and quiet themselves, these people would still not bear any fruits of righteousness while they claim the glory of patience on their part by their neighbor's loss, and are thus altogether removed from that apostolic love that "does not insist on its own way" (1 Cor 13:5) but cares about others. For it does not desire riches in such a way as to make profit for itself out of one's neighbor's loss, nor does it wish to gain anything if it involves the spoiling of another.

IT'S THE STRONG PERSON WHO CAN SUBJECT HIS WILL TO ANOTHER'S

But you must certainly know that, in general, the one who subjects his own will to his brother's plays a stronger part than the one who is found to be the more stubborn in defending and clinging to his own decisions. The former bears and puts up with his neighbor, and so gains the reputation of being strong and vigorous. But the latter gains the reputation of being weak and sickly, someone who must be pampered and petted—so that sometimes for the sake of his peace and quiet it is a good thing to give in a little even in necessary matters.

And indeed by giving in you need not imagine that you have lost anything of your own perfection, though by yielding you have given up something of your intended strictness. On the contrary, you may be sure that you have gained much more by your virtue of long-suffering and patience. For this is the Apostle's command: "We who are strong ought to bear with the failings of the weak" (Rom 15:1), and "Bear one another's burdens, and so fulfil the law of Christ" (Gal 6:2). For a weak man will never support a weak man, nor can one who is suffering in the same way bear or cure one in feeble health. But one who is himself not subject to infirmity brings remedies to one in weak health. For it is rightly said to him, "Physician, heal yourself" (Luke 4:23).

We must note too the fact that, by nature, the weak are quick and ready to offer reproaches and sow the seeds of quarrels, while they themselves cannot bear to be touched by the shadow of the very slightest wrong, and while they are riding roughshod over us and flinging charges right and left, they are not able to bear even the slightest and most trivial ones themselves. And so, according to the aforesaid opinion of the Elders, love cannot last firm and unbroken except among men of the same purpose and goodness. For at some time or other it is sure to be broken, however carefully it may be guarded by one of them.

Germanus. How then can the patience of a perfect man be worthy of praise if it cannot always bear the weak?

Joseph. I did not say that the virtue and endurance of one who is strong and robust would be overcome, but that the miserable condition of the weak, encouraged by the tolerance of the perfect, and daily growing worse, is sure to give rise to reasons on account of which he himself ought no longer to be borne. Otherwise someday, with a shrewd suspicion that the patience of his neighbor shows up and sets off his own impatience, he will choose to go away rather than always to be borne by the magnanimity of the other.

So I think this should be observed above all else by those who want to keep the affection of their companions unimpaired: that first of all, when provoked by any wrongs, a monk should keep not only his lips but even the depth of his breast unmoved. But if he finds that they are even slightly disturbed, let him keep himself in by entire silence, and diligently observe what the Psalmist speaks of: "I was troubled and spoke nothing"; and, "I said, 'I will guard my ways, that I may not sin with my tongue; I will bridle my mouth, so long as the wicked are in my presence.' I was dumb and silent, I held my peace" (Ps 39:1–2). And he should not pay any attention to his present state, or give vent to what his violent rage suggests and his exasperated mind expresses at the moment. Instead, he should dwell on the grace of past love or look forward in his mind to the renewal and restoration of peace and contemplate it even in the very hour of rage, as if it were sure to return soon. And while he is reserving himself for the delight of harmony soon to come, he will not feel the bitterness of the present quarrel and will easily make such answers that, when love is restored, he will not be able to accuse himself as guilty or be blamed by the other. And thus he will fulfill these words of the prophet: "in wrath remember mercy" (Hab 3:2).

How to control your anger

So, then, we should restrain every movement of anger and moderate it under the direction of discretion, so that we may not be hurried by blind rage into that which is condemned by Solomon: "A fool shows all his wrath; but a wise man dispenses it gradually" (Prov 29:11, Septuagint). That is, a fool is inflamed by the passion of his anger to avenge himself; but a wise man diminishes it bit by bit by the ripeness of his counsel and moderation and gets rid of it.

Something of the same kind too is this which is said by the Apostle: "Revenge not yourselves, my dearly beloved; but give place unto wrath" (Rom 12:19, Douay-Rheims version). That is, do not under the compulsion of wrath proceed to vengeance, but give place to wrath, meaning do not let your hearts be confined in the straits of impatience and cowardice so that, when a fierce storm of passion rises, you cannot endure it; but be enlarged in your hearts, receiving the adverse waves of anger in the wide gulf of that love which suffers all things, bears all things (1 Cor 13:7). And so your mind will be enlarged with wide long-suffering and patience, and will have within it safe recesses of counsel, in which the foul smoke of anger will be received and be diffused and immediately vanish away. Or else the passage may be taken in this way: we give place to wrath, as often as we yield with humble and tranquil mind to the passion of another, and bow to the impatience of the passionate, as if we admitted that we deserved any kind of wrong.

But those who twist the meaning of the perfection of which the Apostle speaks so as to make out that those who give place to anger, who go away from a man in a rage, seem to me not to cut off but rather to encourage the incitement to quarreling. For unless a neighbor's wrath is overcome at once by amends being humbly made, a man provokes rather than avoids it by his flight. And there is something like this that Solomon says: "Be not quick to anger, for anger lodges in the bosom of fools" (Eccl 7:9), and "Enter not hastily into a quarrel, lest you repent at the last" (Prov 25:7, Septuagint). For he does not blame a hasty exhibition of quarreling and anger in such a way as to praise a later one.

In the same way too must this be taken: "The vexation of a fool is known at once, but the prudent man ignores an insult" (Prov 12:16). When he tells us that a shameful outburst of anger ought to be hidden by wise men, he does not mean that, while he blames a speedy outburst of anger, he fails to forbid a later one. No, certainly, if owing to human weakness it does burst forth, he means that it should be hidden for this reason, that while for the moment it is wisely covered up, it may be destroyed forever.

For the nature of anger is such that when it is given room it languishes and perishes, but if openly exhibited, it burns more and more. So our hearts should be enlarged and opened wide. Otherwise they might be confined in the narrow straits of cowardice, and be filled with the swelling surge of wrath, and so we become unable to receive what the prophet calls the "exceedingly broad" commandment (Ps 119:96) of God in our narrow heart, or to say with the prophet, "I will run in the way of thy commandments when you enlarge my understanding" (Ps 119:32).

Very clear passages of Scripture teach us that patience is wisdom. "He who is slow to anger has great understanding, but he who has a hasty temper exalts folly" (Prov 14:29). And therefore Scripture says of him who to his credit asked the gift of wisdom from the Lord, "God gave Solomon wisdom and understanding beyond measure, and largeness of mind like the sand on the seashore" (1 Kgs 4:29).

A FRIENDSHIP FOR BAD PURPOSES WON'T LAST

This too has been often proved by many experiments: those who entered the bonds of friendship as part of a conspiracy cannot possibly preserve their harmony unbroken—either because they tried to keep it not out of their desire for perfection nor because of the sway of Apostolic love, but out of earthly love, and because of their wants and the bonds of their agreement; or else because that most crafty foe of ours hurries them on all the faster to break the chains of their friendship in order that he may make them breakers of their oath. This opinion then of the most prudent men is most certainly established: that true harmony and undivided union can only exist among those whose life is pure, and who are men of the same goodness and purpose.

This was what the blessed Joseph said in his spiritual talk on friendship, and he fired us with a more ardent desire to preserve the love of our fellowship as a lasting one.

—John Cassian, Conference 16

10.

BOETHIUS

Boethius—known in the Church as St. Severinus Boethius—comes at the very end of the classical age. The Roman Empire had already fallen in the West, but hardly anyone had noticed yet. Boethius was a minister of the Ostrogothic king of Italy, Theodoric, who technically ruled under the authority of the Roman Emperor way over in Constantinople—an arrangement that worked because the Roman Emperor never tried to exercise that authority.

Theodoric got cranky and paranoid in his old age, seeing conspiracies everywhere. (To be fair to him, there *were* conspiracies everywhere.) Some of the people Boethius trusted as his friends accused him of treason, and the king shut him up in prison. While he was there, Boethius wrote the last gasp of great classical literature: *The Consolation of Philosophy,* a kind of satirical dialogue in prose and verse in which personified Philosophy visits him in his cell to console him.

Ultimately Boethius was executed for treason. His execution guaranteed that the civilized world would largely forget all the accomplishments of Theodoric and remember him only as the man who killed the author of *The Consolation of Philosophy.*

The odd thing about the book is that there's nothing specifically Christian about it—and yet Christians of all times afterward have instantly recognized the workings of a thoroughly Christian mind.

In this passage, Philosophy tells Boethius that Bad Fortune is actually better than Good Fortune. Why? Because Good Fortune always tells you lies, and Bad Fortune always tells the truth. Specifically, only Bad Fortune tells you who your friends really are.

But do not think that I wage implacable war against Fortune. I admit there is a time when the deceitful goddess serves men well—I mean when she reveals herself, uncovers her face, and confesses her true character.

Perhaps you do not understand me yet. This is a strange thing I am trying to express, and for that reason I can hardly find words to make my thought clear. I really do believe that Bad Fortune is of more use to us than Good Fortune. For Good Fortune, when she wears the guise of happiness, and most seems to caress, is always lying; Bad Fortune is always truthful, since, in changing, she shows her inconstancy. The one deceives, the other teaches; the one enchains the minds of those who enjoy her favor by the illusion of good, the other delivers them by the knowledge of the frail nature of happiness.

So you see how the one is fickle, shifting as the breeze, and always self-deceived; the other sober-minded, alert, and wary, by reason of the very discipline of adversity.

Finally, Good Fortune, by her allurements, draws us far

from the true good; Bad Fortune often draws us back to true good with grappling irons.

Again, do you think it is completely worthless that this cruel, this odious Fortune has shown you the hearts of your faithful friends? Good Fortune hid the faces of the true friends and the false alike from you, but in departing she has taken away *her* friends, and left you *yours*. Is there any price you would not have given for this service at the height of your prosperity, when you thought you were fortunate? Cease, then, to seek the wealth you have lost, since in true friends you have found the most precious of all riches.

—Boethius, *Consolation of Philosophy* 2.7

Later on, Philosophy reminds Boethius of the dangers of making friends with the powerful—dangers he knew all too well. But the dangers are just as bad in the other direction. People in power must keep an eye on their friends: "Anyone who has been made a friend by good fortune will be made an enemy by ill fortune."

Well, then, does sovereignty and the intimacy of kings turn out to be able to confer power? Why, surely does not the happiness of kings endure forever? And yet antiquity is full of examples, and these days also, of kings whose happiness has turned into calamity. How glorious a power, which is not even found effectual for its own preservation!

But if happiness has its source in sovereign power, is not

happiness diminished, and misery inflicted in its stead, just so far as that power falls short of completeness? Yet, however widely human sovereignty be extended, there must still be more nations left, over whom each particular king holds no sway. Now, at whatever point the power on which happiness depends ceases, here powerlessness steals in and makes wretchedness; so, by this way of reckoning, there must be a balance of wretchedness in the lot of the king. The tyrant who had experienced the perils of his condition imagined the fears that haunt a throne as a sword hanging over a man's head.[1]

What sort of power, then, is this, if it cannot drive away the gnawings of anxiety, or shun the stings of terror? They wish to live secure themselves, but they cannot—then they boast about their power! Do you really think they have power when you see that they wish for what they cannot make happen? Do you think someone has power when he surrounds himself with a bodyguard, when he fears those he terrifies more than they fear him, when to keep up the appearance of power he is himself at the mercy of his slaves?

Need I say anything of the friends of kings, when I show royal dominion itself so utterly and miserably weak? Often the royal power in its abundance brings them low; often it involves them in its fall. Nero forced his friend and preceptor, Seneca, to choose how he would die. Antoninus exposed Papinianus, who was long powerful at court, to the swords

---

[1] This is the story of the Sword of Damocles. The legend is that the flattering Damocles kept telling the tyrant Dionysius of Syracuse how lucky he was, until Dionysius offered to switch places for a day. Damocles sat on the throne, but Dionysius had a sword suspended above him by a single horsehair. That, he explained, is what it's like to be as fortunate as I am.

of the soldiery. Yet each of these was willing to renounce his power. Seneca tried to surrender his wealth also to Nero and go into retirement; but neither achieved his purpose. When they tottered, their very greatness dragged them down.

What kind of thing, then, is this power that keeps men in fear while they possess it? When you want to keep it, you are not safe, and when you want to set it aside you cannot get rid of it! Are friends any protection who have been attached by fortune, not by virtue? No! Anyone who has been made a friend by good fortune will be made an enemy by bad fortune. And what plague is more effective at hurting you than a foe of your own household?

—Boethius, *Consolation of Philosophy* 2.5

11.

GREGORY THE GREAT

By now we've certainly established that friends are good to have. Life is hardly worthwhile without them.

But it's also true that friends can sometimes lead us in the wrong direction. Anyone who's ever been young and foolish (in other words, any human being) can remember being led into stupid behavior by friends. As we've already seen, once Christians became the majority, the Fathers tended to shift from praising the glories of friendship to warning of the temptations bad friends can bring along with them.

Usually we think of those temptations in terms of obvious sins—like fraternity parties. But there are some less obvious temptations friends can lead us into.

When we think of friends in the Old Testament, we probably think of the famous friendships of David and Jonathan, or Ruth and Naomi. But the friends who get the most attention, if we judge simply by word count, are the friends of Job.

Some friends they were! That's our first reaction. And yet they were doing their honest best to help Job in his time of trouble. They were just doing it wrong.

In fact, St. Gregory the Great (who died in 604) sees the friends of Job as another affliction of the devil. After remarking how Satan's attempts to bring Job to curse God only made him a better example to all of us, Gregory tells us that Satan brings on Job's friends as a new and worse temptation.

For us, Gregory says, Job's friends represent heretics, who try to lead us away from the Church to follow their own incorrect notions of God. But even these false friends can be brought back to the Church by our prayers, just as the friends of Job were brought back into good standing by Job's prayers.

The ancient enemy, therefore, because he was grieved at being foiled by him in his domestic trials, proceeded to seek for help from abroad. He therefore summoned Job's friends, each from his own place, as if for the purpose of displaying their affection, and opened their lips, under the pretense of giving consolation. But, by these very means, he launched against him shafts of reproach, which would wound more severely the heart of him who securely listened to them, because they were inflicting an unexpected wound beneath the cover of a friendship which was professed and not observed.

After these, also, Elihu, a younger person, is urged on even to use insult, in order that the scornful levity of his youth might at all events disturb the tranquility of such great gentleness.

But against these many machinations of the ancient enemy, Job's constancy stood unconquered, his equanimity unbroken. At one and the same time he opposed his prudence to their hostile words, and his conduct to their doings.

It was expressly written of Job after his scourging, "In all this Job did not sin or charge God with wrong" (Job 1:22).

But let no one suppose that this holy man sinned afterwards either, at least in his words in his dispute with his friends. For Satan meant to tempt him, but God, who had praised him, took on himself the significance of that contest. So if anyone complains that blessed Job sinned in his words, he can only be saying that God, who pledged himself for him, had been the loser! . . .

But his friends, who are railing against him while pretending to advise, represent to us *heretics*, who under the pretense of advising, carry on the business of leading us astray. And thus while speaking to Job on behalf of the Lord, they hear the Lord's reproof—because all heretics, though they mean to maintain God's cause, are actually offending him.

Thus this same holy man is right to say to them, "I desire to reason with God, having first shewn that you are forgers of lies, and maintainers of perverse opinions" (Job 13:3–4, Douay-Rheims version). It is plain then that they typify heretics, since the holy man accuses them of being "maintainers of perverse opinions." And since Job is by interpretation *grieving* (for by his grief is set forth either the passion of the Mediator, or the struggles of the Holy Church, which is harassed by the manifold labors of this present life), so do his friends also by the very word which is used for their names set forth the nature of their conduct.

Eliphaz signifies in Latin *contempt of God*—and what else is the conduct of heretics than a proud *contempt of God* by the false notions they entertain of him?

Bildad is interpreted *oldness alone*. And well are all heretics termed *oldness alone*, in the things they speak of God, since they are anxious to appear preachers, not with any honest intention, but with an earnest desire after worldly honor. For they are urged to speak not by the zeal of the new man, but by the evil principles of their *old life*.

Sophar too is called in Latin *dissipation of the prospect*, or a *dissipating of the prospect*. For the minds of the faithful raise themselves to the contemplation of things above: but when the words of the heretics endeavor to draw them aside from the right objects of contemplation, they do their best to *dissipate the prospect*.

In the three names then of Job's friends, there are set forth three cases of the ruin of heretics. If they did not despise God, they would never entertain false notions respecting him; and did they not contract oldness, they would not go wrong in their estimate of the new life; and unless they marred the contemplation of the good, the divine judgments would not have reproved them with so strict a scrutiny for the faults which they committed in their words. By despising God then, they keep themselves in their oldness: but by remaining in their oldness, they obstruct the view of them that are right by their crooked discoursing.

But what is meant by the Divine Voice directing that the three friends should be reconciled by seven sacrifices, while it leaves Elihu only beneath the reproof of a single sentence? It must be that heretics, when sprinkled with the superabundance of divine grace, sometimes return to the unity of the Holy Church. This is excellently set forth by the very reconciliation of the friends, for whom nevertheless blessed Job is directed to pray. Because in truth the sacrifices of heretics cannot be acceptable to God unless they are offered for them by the hands of the Catholic Church, that they may gain a healing remedy by the merits of the Church they used to attack with the shafts of their reproaches.

This is why seven sacrifices are said to have been offered for them, because while they receive on confession the Spirit of sevenfold grace, they are atoned for, as it were, by seven oblations. Thus in the Apocalypse of John, the whole Church is represented by the sevenfold number of the Churches (Rev 1:11), and hence is it that Solomon speaks thus of Wisdom, "Wisdom has built her house, she has set up her seven pillars" (Prov 9:1). The heretics then on their reconciliation express, by the very number of the sacrifices, their own former character, since it is only by their returning that they are united to the perfection of sevenfold grace.

But they are properly represented as having offered for themselves bulls and rams. For in a bull is designated the neck of pride, in a ram the leading of the flocks that follow. What then is the offering of bulls and rams on their behalf, but the destruction of their proud leadership, that they may think humbly of themselves, and not seduce any longer the hearts of the innocent to follow them? For they had started aside with swelling neck from the general body of the Church, and were leading after them the weak-minded, as flocks following their guidance. Let them come then to blessed Job—that is, let them return to the Church, and offer bulls and rams to be slaughtered for a sevenfold sacrifice, who in order to be united to the Catholic Church, by the coming in of a spirit of humility, have to put an end to whatever swelling thoughts they used to entertain from their haughty leadership.

—Gregory the Great, *Moralia* 23

12.

ISIDORE OF SEVILLE

Poor Isidore was a man who deserved better times to live in. He was meant to be the sort of squirrelly old scholar who spends his days among piles of books discovering wonderful new tracks through the writings of the ancients.

And, in fact, he spent as much of his life that way as he could. Thanks to Isidore's insatiable collecting, we have bits and pieces of ancient authors whose works would otherwise have vanished.

But Isidore lived in one of the darkest times for civilization in Europe. He was born in 560 into a world where the Roman Empire had collapsed, and no one knew what to do with all the scattered pieces. Literacy was rare and literature was rarer. In a long and active life, Isidore found himself called on to participate in some of the great political upheavals of his time. Most notably, he was one of the main forces behind the conversion of the Visigothic kings of Spain from Arianism to orthodox Catholic Christianity.

Still, he found time to write books—lots of books. We commonly call Isidore the last of the Latin Fathers, and he did his best to preserve what was left of the great Christian classical civilization that gave us Ambrose and Augustine.

One of his books is usually called the *Sentences*, because the Latin title is *Sententiarum libri III* (the *Three Books of Sententiae*). A simpler and better translation would be *Thoughts*. It's a collection of Isidore's scattered thoughts, collected under various subject headings. A few chapters are devoted to the subject of friendship, and here Isidore seems to distill all the teachings of the earlier Fathers into a few choice words. Real friendship can only exist among the good. False friends are revealed by adversity. Only selfless friendship is lasting. We've heard these ideas from all the writers before. But Isidore adds a few interesting ideas of his own, as we'll see.

On false friends

A deceitful friend is quickly exposed by adversity. For friendship is uncertain in prosperity: we do not know whether our friends love us or our good fortune.

Often friendship is cultivated by hypocrisy, so that one who cannot openly trap us may trap us by deceit.

Anyone who despises a friend struck by some adversity is going against divine piety and justice. By doing so he both destroys his own chance of a reward and makes the blow to his neighbor all the crueler—as happened with ulcerous Lazarus and the proud rich man (see Luke 16:19–31). Through adversity and prosperity, therefore, it is proved whether people really love God and their neighbors. For adversity detects our deceitful friends: the one who pretended to love us immediately despises us.

No force can end an established friendship; no time can abolish it; for even where time turns everything upside-down, friendship remains steadfast.

Rare are the friends who remain dear to the end. Many are diverted from charity either by bad times or by an argument over some silly thing one of them has done.

Even the morals of some people are changed by worldly success, and those who once held their associates dear, having reached the pinnacle of success, scorn to have friends.

On friendship based on benefit

Among true friends, friendship is born of goodwill; false ones come together for benefit.

Those who are joined by benefit rather than grace are not faithful in friendship. For they will quickly desert unless they keep receiving benefits forever. An attachment created by benefit is dissolved when the benefit ceases. True friendship is the kind that asks for nothing that belongs to the friend except his goodwill—which is to say, the kind that freely loves the lover.

Most often friendship is born from necessity or poverty, so that each may get what he wants from the other. The one who truly seeks friendship is the one who desires it when he needs nothing. For friendship from poverty is short and tainted; when it is pure, it is perpetual.

ON THE COMPANIONSHIP OF THE WICKED

We should have friendship in good things only; for those who use friendship for wicked purposes become not our friends but our enemies.

The companionship of the wicked is opposed to that of the good. And just as we should wish for the good to have peace with each other, so we should wish for the wicked to have discord. Indeed, Paul the Apostle demonstrates that the unanimity of the wicked is opposed to that of the good: he divided the wicked against themselves when he saw them conspiring to kill him (see Acts 23:6–10). Thus in the Law, in the Red Sea, the agreement of the wicked was divided, so that the way of the chosen people toward happiness would not be blocked. The way of the good is blocked, however, if the sea—that is, the unity of the wicked—is not divided.

—Isidore of Seville, *Sentences* 3.29–31 (new translation)

Isidore's own best friend was Braulio, who moved away and left Isidore missing him terribly, to judge by this letter. He missed his friend so much that he even sent Braulio gifts, in a way that was uniquely characteristic of Isidore. Of all the works Isidore wrote, the one he's most known for is his *Etymologies,* an encyclopedia of all world knowledge based on fanciful ideas of word origins. In our time, etymology is a science based on comparative linguistics. In ancient times, it was a kind of word game based on elaborate puns: this word *sounds* like that one, so the one must have come from the other, and how appropriate the meaning is! In this letter, we see that Isidore's irrepressible instinct for punning even spilled over into physical objects, like the gifts he sent his absent friend.

ISIDORE TO HIS DEAREST AND MOST BELOVED SON IN CHRIST, BRAULIO THE ARCHDEACON

When you get a letter from a friend, my dearest son, do not hesitate to embrace it as a friend. For it is a fortunate consolation to those who are separated that, if the beloved is not present, a letter can be embraced in his place. I have sent you a ring (*annulum*) for my heart (*animum*),[1] and a mantle as a cloak (*amictus*) for our friendship (*amicitia*), which is where the ancients got that word. So pray for me, that the Lord may inspire you, so that I may earn the reward of seeing you here while I still live, and you may make the one whom your departure made unhappy happy again by showing yourself once more. I have sent a pamphlet of rules to you by way of Maurentio the primicerius. As for the rest, I always want to know about your health, my most beloved lord and dearest son.

—Isidore, Letter 2 (new translation)

---

[1] These two words would have looked very similar in the writing of Isidore's time.

13.

RABANUS MAURUS

RABANUS MAURUS lived at what must have been a very exciting time in history.

After the Roman Empire fizzled out in the West, civilization was hanging by a thread. Only the monasteries kept literacy alive.

But then came Charlemagne.

Charles the Great—Carolus Magnus in Latin—was King of the Franks, the largest kingdom in western Europe at the time. He might have been an illiterate barbarian, but he had big plans. He conquered more territory than had been held under one government since the Roman Empire, and he wanted nothing less than to restore civilization. He even learned to read a bit himself, although writing always gave him fits, and he had to trace the letters carefully with a stencil. In the year 800, after Charles had already been the great power in the West for many years, the pope crowned him Roman Emperor.

During his long and prosperous reign, Charlemagne gathered all the most brilliant scholars in western Europe and set them the task of reviving culture. His scholar-in-chief, Alcuin, promoted a legible manuscript style that forms the basis of the printed lower-case letters in this book. (We call it "Carolingian minuscule," because even though he could hardly write, King Carolus Magnus gets naming rights.)

One of the most brilliant of those literary lights—and Alcuin's favorite student—was St. Rabanus Maurus (his name is also spelled Rhabanus or Hrabanus). He wrote a huge number of commentaries on Scripture, as well as some technically brilliant poems (one famously in the shape of a cross) and the hymn *Veni Creator Spiritus,* which Catholics still use today.

His commentary on Sirach gave Rabanus a chance to weigh in on the idea of friendship. There's a famous passage about friendship in Sirach 6 that runs this way in the Revised Standard Version:

> When you gain a friend, gain him through testing, and do not trust him hastily. For there is a friend who is such at his own convenience, but will not stand by you in your day of trouble. And there is a friend who changes into an enemy, and will disclose a quarrel to your disgrace. And there is a friend who is a table companion, but will not stand by you in your day of trouble. In your prosperity he will make himself your equal, and be bold with your servants; but if you are brought low he will turn against you, and will hide himself from your presence. Keep yourself far from your enemies, and be on guard toward your friends.
>
> A faithful friend is a sturdy shelter: he that has found one has found a treasure. There is nothing so precious as a faithful friend, and no scales can measure his excellence. A faithful friend is an elixir

of life; and those who fear the Lord will find him. Whoever fears the Lord directs his friendship aright, for as he is, so is his neighbor also. (Sir 6:7–17)

All the passages from Sirach in Rabanus' commentary below are from the Douay-Rheims version, which is translated from the Vulgate text that Rabanus used. The manuscripts he read didn't have our modern apparatus of punctuation, so sometimes Rabanus makes different decisions about where sentences begin and end; in those cases, the quotations are altered to fit Rabanus' interpretation.

It seems that Rabanus' commentary on Sirach has never been translated into English before, so this is very likely the first time you've read it. But it won't be the first time for *all* of it. It's often hard to tell how much of Rabanus' commentary is his own. He had a habit of dropping in whole passages from the earlier Fathers without attribution, and scholars are still identifying those quotations in his work. Rabanus' normal mode of working was to collect everything good and place it where it was most needed to explain Scripture. That made his commentaries tremendously useful in his day. But pity the modern scholars who look for clues to Rabanus' life in his writings! They must be very careful not to build up some fantastic Frankenstein's monster out of bits and pieces of all the Fathers.

The beginning of this passage gives Rabanus a chance to discuss the difference between false and true friends. According to Rabanus, the sacred writer spends so much time describing false friends precisely because, by doing so, he draws an outline of what a true friend looks like.

"If you would get a friend, try him before you take him, and do not credit him easily. For there is a friend for his own occasion, and he will not abide in the day of your trouble. And there is a friend that turns to enmity; and there is a friend that will disclose hatred and strife and reproaches. And there is a friend a companion at the table, and he will not abide in the day of distress. A friend, if he continues steadfast, shall be to you as yourself, and shall act with confidence among them of your household" (Sir 6:7–11).

He describes false friends in various ways, thus arriving at a demonstration of what a true friend is. Many will profess to be your friends in prosperity, and in adversity turn out to be your enemies. So he adds, "If he humbles himself before you, and hides himself from your face" (Sir 6:12). For he pretends to be devoted to you, but when you need him most he shows that his heart is quite otherwise. That is what it means when it says "hides himself": that is, he pretends to be what he is not.

"You shall have unanimous friendship for good. Separate yourself from your enemies, and take heed of your friends" (Sir 6:12–13). When there is unanimity between friends, the friendship is long-lasting. But when it is a fiction and not the truth, there is no stability in the friendship. Thus he warns that where they are subject to enmity, they should separate themselves, and use caution in discerning their friends. We should note, however, that this kind of discretion is most necessary between Catholics and heretics, because heretics hypocritically make use of all their wiles so that they may deceive the careless more easily. Thus the Savior warns us in the Gospel: "Beware of false prophets, who come to you in the clothing of sheep, but inwardly they are ravening wolves. By their fruits you shall know them," and so on (Matt 7:15–16). . . .

"A faithful friend is a strong defense: and he who has found him, has found a treasure. Nothing can be compared to a faithful friend, and no weight of gold and silver is able to countervail the goodness of his fidelity" (Sir 6:14–15).

To interpret this famous passage, Rabanus adopts the words of Ambrose—the words we already read earlier, lightly edited. He does so without attributing them to Ambrose, and a modern university professor would give him an F for plagiarism. But "plagiarism" would have been a foreign idea to Rabanus. Books were scarce in his time, and Charlemagne's pet scholars were engaged in an all-out effort to preserve what was good in the culture. Taking what was good from Ambrose and putting it in his commentary was Rabanus' way of making those valuable thoughts available to other Christian scholars. (In fact, Ambrose did the same thing to Origen—and St. Jerome accused Ambrose of plagiarism. But that was a different literary world, before the collapse of classical civilization.)

"A faithful friend is the medicine of life and immortality: and they that fear the Lord, shall find him" (Sir 6:14–16).

Interpreting this verse, Rabanus pulls in a favorite etymology of "friend" that goes back at least to Gregory the Great, and then gives us a long quotation from Cicero. Then he immediately slips into St. John Cassian's numbered list of the steps to perfect friendship. Again, he passes along what's good in the culture, even pre-Christian culture:

Amicus ("friend") is said as if it were *animi custos* ("guardian of the soul"). Certainly in a faithful friend there is medicine of life and immortality: because if he is faithful, he is certainly a friend according to God; and if he is a friend according to God, he is always heading with his friend toward the things that have to do with the medicines of eternal life and perpetual immortality. Thus this sentiment from Tullius Cicero, "that true friendship can only be found among the virtuous. For in the first place, sincerity is so essential a quality in forming a good, or, if you please, a wise, man (for they are convertible terms), that a person of that character would deem it more generous to be a declared enemy, than to conceal a rancorous heart under a smooth brow; and in the next, the same generous simplicity of heart would not only induce him to vindicate his friend against the accusation of others, but render him incapable of cherishing in his own breast that little suspicious temper, which is ever apt to take offense, and perpetually discovering some imaginary violation of amity. Add to this, that his conversation and address ought to be sweetened with a certain ease and politeness of language and manners, that wonderfully contribute to heighten and improve the relish of this intercourse. A solemn, severe demeanor may be very proper, I confess, in certain characters, to give them their proper impression; but friendship should wear a more pleasing aspect, and at all times appear with a complacent, affable, and unconstrained countenance."[1]

"He who fears God shall likewise have good friendship: because according to him shall his friend be" (Sir 6:17).

Therefore the full and perfect grace of friendship cannot persist except among perfect individuals, the holy Fathers have taught. Thus we can reach the goal of perfect and permanent friendship by following these steps they have given us:

1. The first step of true friendship, they say, is to have contempt of the things of this world and disdain for all the things we own.

2. The second is that both friends should restrain their wills, so that neither, thinking himself wise or clever, prefers to follow his own decisions rather than his neighbor's.

3. Third, you should know that all things, even those we think useful or necessary, are secondary to the good of charity and peace.

4. Fourth, you should believe that nothing justifies harboring anger, whether just or unjust.

5. Fifth, you should desire to cure your brother's annoyance, even if it there was no good reason for it, in the same way you desire to cure your own—knowing that the other's vexation is as important to you as your own, and you may be

---

[1]   The quotation is from *Laelius,* 65 (translated by Melmoth, 98–100).

angry with someone else unless you drive the anger from your brother's mind as well as you can.

6. Finally, what is doubtless fatal to all vices in general: you should believe every day that you are about to leave this world—a persuasion that will not only allow no melancholy to linger in your heart, but also curb all movements of concupiscence and sin.

Whoever keeps these precepts, therefore, can neither suffer nor cause the bitterness of anger and strife.

—Rabanus Maurus, Commentary on Sirach 2.2

14.

CONCLUSION: THIRD-CENTURY SOLUTIONS TO A TWENTY-FIRST-CENTURY PROBLEM

WHEN WE STARTED this tour through the Fathers, we noted two phases in their writings on friendship.

The first phase was back when Christianity was still an illegal cult practiced by a minority in the Roman Empire—a rapidly growing minority, but still a minority. In those days the main concern was spreading the Good News, because clearly the world needed it. So the emphasis was on bringing God's friendship out into the world through our friendships with our neighbors.

The second phase came after Constantine made Christianity the favored religion of the Empire. With Christians—at least nominal Christians—on top now, Christian writers began to be worried more about the dangers of bad company.

That isn't a hard and fast distinction. The very first

Christian writer—Paul—warned the Corinthians that "Bad company ruins good morals" (1 Cor 15:33). He was quoting the comic playwright Menander, who in turn was just writing down what every parent of a teenager has said every night since the dawn of humanity. And on the other hand, we saw how lyrically and heartbreakingly Augustine wrote about the joys of friendship and the grief of loss. But it's a broad pattern.

And it makes sense. In a world where it was illegal to be a Christian—a death-penalty offense, in fact—you could probably count on most Christians being committed to the faith. Just because they already had to make so many sacrifices to be a Christian, they would be much more likely to be on the alert for bad influences.

On the other hand, in a world where Christianity was the norm, most nominal Christians were just passing through life without a firm commitment to the faith. They didn't have to make a hard choice to be Christian. It was just what happened when you didn't make a choice. So their leaders—the preachers and bishops of the Church—had to watch out for them. They had to remind their flock of the dangers that surrounded them.

For most of the rest of Western history, from then until very recently, that's been the case. Through the Middle Ages and the Renaissance, Europe was Christian. Just by being born, you had found your way into the Christian Church. But that didn't mean you were a committed Christian. All the thieves and gamblers and drunks you met were baptized Christians, too. Isidore of Seville, as you remember, felt it was worthwhile to devote a whole chapter to the supposed friendships of criminals, and how they differed from real friendships.

The Reformation was a serious challenge to Christian unity, but it wasn't until the French Revolution that there was an avowedly anti-Christian force strong enough to present a serious challenge to Christianity itself. Even that seemed to be a temporary anomaly: after the dust settled, Napoleon made a deal with the Church, and France was Catholic again.

But the twentieth century saw one attempt after another to stamp out the Christian religion in whole societies. Communism was officially atheist. Fascism was happy to take the support of naïve Christians for the time being, but only because there were too many of them to kill all at once.

Even where there was no official interference with religion, intellectual fashions turned virulently anti-Christian. Pop culture followed soon enough. If you formed your opinion of Western society from Hollywood, you might be forgiven for thinking that Christians were some weird little minority obsessed with bringing back the Inquisition.

The West is only a small part of the world, of course. In the larger picture, Christianity is growing fast, and more of the world is Christian every day.

But in the West, many of us live in a world where Christianity can no longer be taken for granted. In fact, depending on where we live or work, we may live in a world where most people are as fantastically ignorant of Christianity as Caecilius, the pagan friend of Minucius Felix who thought Christians had baby-eating orgies every night.

In other words, for many of us, the world is back where it was before Constantine. Being Christian is no longer the easy road. It takes commitment.

And if we're going to rescue our neighbors from their loneliness and despair, we have to exercise the virtue of friendship. We must be *heroic* friends.

So how do we exercise that virtue? How do we broadcast the friendship of God in a world that doesn't want to listen to any of that God stuff?

First of all, we have to make a conscious decision that we're going to be *Christian* friends. That means rejecting Cicero's definition of friendship right off the bat. We can't *allow* ourselves to be friends only with people who agree with us on everything.

Think of Minucius Felix and his friend Octavius. They weren't going to reject their friend Caecilius just because he wasn't a Christian, just because he held their religion in contempt, just because he *theoretically* believed that they deserved death for it.

But on the other hand, they also weren't going to leave him in ignorance without letting him know the truth they had discovered. Their friendship was too good for that. They wanted Caecilius to have that truth, too, because friends want the best for their friends.

They were good enough friends that they were confident their friendship could survive a vigorous debate. In fact, they were confident that it would be all the better for it. And in this case it worked: the non-Christian was converted.

What happens when it doesn't work? What happens when people call us names, shout at us, tell us we're what's wrong with the world?

Well, Jesus prepared us for that. "Blessed are you when men revile you and persecute you and utter all kinds of evil against you falsely on my account. Rejoice and be glad, for your reward is great in heaven, for so men persecuted the prophets who were before you" (Matt 5:11–12).

Sometimes being a good friend isn't possible, because the other person just won't allow it. But we got some good advice from St. John Chrysostom: "But, look, you will say, I am trying to be friends, but the others aren't! Well, all the greater the reward to you." And then he reminds us that we probably haven't *really* tried yet.

Meanwhile, we can't neglect our Christian friends. The world is always full of temptations, but it seems that our technological society specializes in producing temptation on an industrial scale. So don't forget the words of Chrysostom: "For a while, by whatever means, keep him away from his evil practice; let him get used to not going off to that pit, whether through you or through any other means. When you have got him used to not going, then by taking him after he has caught his breath a little you will be able to teach him that he ought to do this for God's sake, and not for man's. Don't try to fix everything at once, since you can't: but do it gently and by degrees."

We've read enough of the Fathers on friendship to know that they don't always agree. Take the most brilliant minds from the most brilliant ages of Christian history, and you're certain to get a debate. But if there's one thing all the Fathers agree on, it's that friendship is a virtue, and like the other virtues, it needs work. It isn't just a nice thing that falls into your lap. If you want friends, you must put in the effort of *being* a friend.

But the effort is worth it. "Great wisdom, to be able to be a creator of friendship!" said Chrysostom. "Take away friendship, and you have taken away all, you have confounded all."

In a lonely society, Christians can be the creators of friendship. We can do it because Christ himself made us his friends, and with his grace comes the miraculous power to spread that friendship all through the world. We saw how the early Christians did it in a world that was more hostile than ours. All we must do is realize that friendship is important, that it takes work, and that the God who has called us friends is ready to help us.

BIBLIOGRAPHY

Unless otherwise listed, the texts of the Fathers come from the *Ante-Nicene Fathers* and the *Nicene and Post-Nicene Fathers*.

Augustine. *The City of God*. In *The Works of Aurelius Augustine, Bishop of Hippo,* edited by the Rev. Marcus Dods. Edinburgh: T. & T. Clark, 1871.

Augustine. *St. Augustine's Confessions: or, Praises of God*. Newly translated into English from the original Latin. Dublin: Richard Cross, 1770. (The uncredited translator, according to other sources, is Richard Challoner.)

Boethius. *The Consolation of Philosophy of Boethius*. Translated into English Prose and Verse by H. R. James. London: Elliot Stock, 1897.

Carola, Joseph. *Augustine of Hippo: The Role of the Laity in Ecclesial Reconciliation*. Rome: Editrice Pontificia Università Gregoriana, 2005.

Cicero. *Cato and Laelius: or, Essays on Old-Age and Friendship*. With remarks by William Melmoth, Esq. London: J. Dodsley, 1795.

Isidore of Seville. *Sententiarum Libri III* and *Epistolae*. In *S. Isidori Hispalensis Episcopi Opera Omnia,* Tomus VI. Edited by Franciso Lorenzana. Rome: Antonio Fulgonio, 1797.

Lienhard, Joseph T. "Friendship in Paulinus of Nola and Augustine." *Augustiniana* 40, nos. 1–4 (1990).

Nawar, Tamer. "Augustine on the Dangers of Friendship." *The Classical Quarterly* 65, no. 2 (December 2015): 836-851.

Newman, John Henry. *The Church of the Fathers*. London: J. G. F. & J. Rivington, 1842.

Rabanus Maurus. *Commentariorum in Ecclesiasticum Libri Decem*. In *B. Rabani Mauri Opera Omnia*, Tomus Tertius. Edited by J.-P. Migne. Paris: J.-P. Migne, 1864.